Sew Adorable

Sew Adorable

classic clothes for boys and girls

Vanessa Mooncie

First published 2014 by
Guild of Master Craftsman Publications Ltd
Castle Place, 166 High Street, Lewes,
East Sussex BN7 1XU

ISBN 978 1 86108 931 1

A catalogue record for this book is available from the
British Library.

Publisher Jonathan Bailey
Production Manager Jim Bulley
Managing Editor Gerrie Purcell
Senior Project Editors Virginia Brehaut and Sara Harper
Editor Cath Senker
Managing Art Editor Gilda Pacitti
Art Editor Rebecca Mothersole
Photographers Richard Boll, Chris Gloag
and Rebecca Mothersole

Set in Century BT
Colour origination by GMC Reprographics
Printed and bound in China

Contents

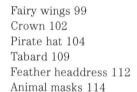

Introduction

The arrival of a new baby inspires a flurry of creativity and there is nothing nicer than a personal token made with love and care. Sewing children's clothing is far simpler than making a garment for an adult. There are less fitting issues and the proportions are smaller, making the whole project quicker and easier. This book contains 23 projects: a range of garments, dressing-up costumes and accessories for ages 0–3 years, all with illustrated step-by-step instructions. The Techniques section at the back of the book will equip you with all you need to know to create each project.

A soft pair of baby boots or appliquéd bib will make a perfect gift to welcome a newborn. The novelty of creating something special and unique for a cherished little one does not wear off, but grows with the child. In the summer months, the perfect attire for days spent building sandcastles and picnicking at the seaside can simply be a roomy romper and a wide-brimmed hat. As the baby grows and starts to express their own creativity, the play apron will protect clothing from the inevitable splashes of paint, and the functional divided front pocket is perfect for keeping brushes and pencils close to hand. In the cooler months, a new coat with its Peter Pan collar will keep them cosy and the inside pocket is a perfect place to hide a shiny conker they might find on an autumn day. Red Riding Hood may have worn a similar style to the cape in soft, red felted wool, to visit her grandmother.

As the child journeys into the imaginative world of play, dressing up only enhances the adventure of a mystical fairy or brave knight. Animal masks will transform them into a fox, rabbit or cat and a pirate hat will take them on numerous seafaring escapades. Any remnant of fabric left over from a project need not go to waste, but can be used to make the dolls or toy rabbit – all ideal companions to snuggle up with at bedtime after a busy day of play.

The fabrics you choose should be hardwearing and easy to launder. With such a choice of colours and textures available, you can let your own imagination run wild to transform a favourite pattern by sewing it again in a new printed fabric, adding a contrasting lining or applying a stencilled design. I hope you enjoy making these projects as much as I have enjoyed creating them.

Gallery

Inspired by the lovingly made garments
that our grandparents might have worn,
these projects have been created with the
imaginative play of the child in mind.

boy's romper page 58

girl's romper page 58

opposite: **party dress** page 88
above left: **fairy wings** page 99
above right: **dolls** page 122

boy's and girl's pants page 78

dungarees page 74

below: **waistcoat** page 86 **and shorts** page 81
opposite: **coat** page 64

above: **baby boots and shoes** page 135

opposite: **coat** page 64 **and aviator-style hat** page 128

above and opposite: **sun dress** page 70 **and rain hat** page 118
above right: **aviator-style hat** page 128 **and coat** page 64

above and opposite: **pyjamas** page 46
above left: **bib** page 130 **and shoes** page 135

above right: **pyjamas** page 46 **and trousers** page 81
above left: **cape** page 94, **trousers** page 81 **and sun hat** page 118
opposite: **cape** page 94 **and trousers** page 81

opposite: **feather headdress** page 112
above: **animal masks (fox and rabbit)** page 114

play apron page 132

opposite: **sun hat** page 118
above: **animal mask (fox)** page 114 **and bib** page 130

 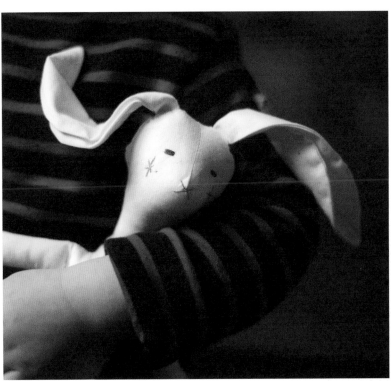

above: **dolls** page 122

opposite: **tabards** page 109 **and animal masks (fox and rabbit)** page 114

above: **tabards** page 109, **long- and short-sleeved shirts** page 52 and **animal masks** page 114
opposite: **long-sleeved shirt** page 52 and **crown** page 102

opposite: **short-sleeved shirt** page 52 **and fox mask** page 114
above: **pirate hat** page 104

The Projects

With carefully chosen fabrics
and the following patterns,
you can create a unique tailored
wardrobe for your children.

pyjamas

These pyjamas are suitable for any season, made in cool shirting or cozy brushed cotton. The pocket can be cut so that the stripes run horizontally to add extra interest.

The following guide shows how much material you will need for an average-sized child.

FABRIC WIDTH (WITHOUT NAP)	1 YEAR OLD	2 YEAR OLD	3 YEAR OLD
36in (90cm)	1³/₈yd (1.3m)	1¹/₂yd (1.4m)	1¹/₂yd (1.4m)
45in (115cm)	1¹/₂yd (1.4m)	1⁵/₈yd (1.5m)	1³/₄yd (1.6m)
60in (150cm)	1¹/₄yd (1.1m)	1¹/₄yd (1.1m)	1¹/₃yd (1.2m)
36in (90cm)-wide lightweight iron-on interfacing	¹/₂yd (0.45m)	²/₃yd (0.6m)	²/₃yd (0.6m)

Suggested fabrics

Cotton shirting, brushed cotton, batiste, lightweight linen, chambray

Sewing notions

- Thread to match fabric
- 4 x ³/₄in (2cm) buttons
- ³/₈in (1cm)-wide elastic to fit the waist comfortably, with an extra ³/₄in (2cm)
- Bodkin or safety pin

Pattern pieces on sheets A and B

1 Back (cut 1 in main fabric)
2 Sleeve (cut 2 in main fabric)
3 Collar (cut 2 in main fabric and 1 in interfacing)
4 Back facing (cut 1 in main fabric)
5 Pocket (cut 2 in main fabric)
6 Front (cut 2 in main fabric and 2 front facings in interfacing)
7 Trousers (cut 2 in main fabric)

Finished measurements

Back length of pyjama top:
1 year: 15¹/₃in (39cm)
2 years: 16¹/₃in (41.5cm)
3 years: 17¹/₃in (44cm)
Side length of pyjama trousers:
1 year: 19³/₄in (50cm)
2 years: 21¹/₄in (54cm)
3 years: 22³/₄in (58cm)

Seam allowances

Take ⁵/₈in (1.5cm) seam allowances throughout, unless otherwise stated.

36in (90cm) wide
SELVEDGES

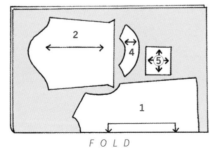

FOLD

36in (90cm) wide
SELVEDGES

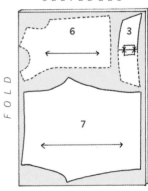

SELVEDGES

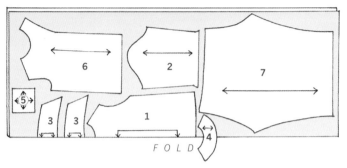

45in (115cm) wide

S E L V E D G E S

F O L D

Open fabric out to cut back facing

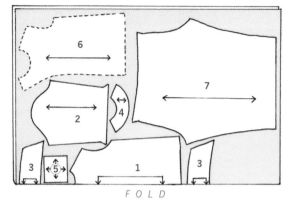

60in (150cm) wide

S E L V E D G E S

F O L D

Broken lines indicate
reverse side of pattern

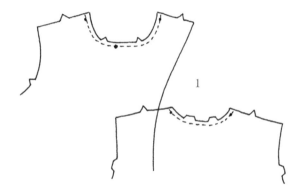

Instructions

Pyjama top

1   Staystitch *(see page 151)* the neck edges of the front
and back pieces to prevent the fabric from stretching.

Join back to front

2   With right sides together, matching notches, pin
and stitch the front pieces to the back at the
shoulder seams.

Key

☐ Right side of fabric

▨ Wrong side of fabric

▨ Interfacing

3

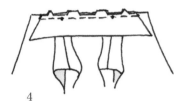

4

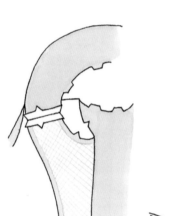

5

Collar and facings

3 Following the manufacturer's instructions, apply iron-on interfacing to the wrong side of one collar piece. This will be the under collar. With right sides together, pin the second collar piece to the under collar. Stitch around the three outer edges, leaving the neck edge open. Trim the seams and cut diagonally across the corners *(see page 153)*. Turn right side out and press.

4 With the right side of the under collar to the right side of the garment, matching notches at the front neck and the dots to the shoulders, pin the neck edges together. Tack the collar in place, stitching through all layers.

5 Following the manufacturer's instructions, apply iron-on interfacing *(see page 145)* to the wrong side of the left and right front facings. Stitch the front facings to the back facing at the shoulder edges. Press the seams open.

6 Turn under and press a ¼in (6mm) hem around the outside edge of the left and right front facings and the back facing. Stitch close to the pressed-under edges.

7 With right sides together, turn the neck edge of the facings at the fold line as indicated on the pattern piece. Matching the notches and shoulder seams, pin and stitch the facings to the garment at the neck edge. Trim the seam, notch the curves and cut diagonally across the corners, taking care not to cut into the stitches.

6

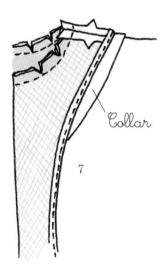

Collar

7

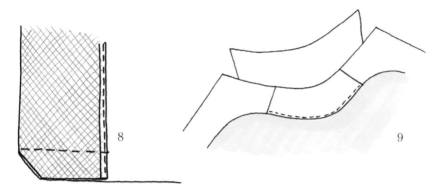

8

9

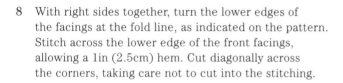

10

8   With right sides together, turn the lower edges of
    the facings at the fold line, as indicated on the pattern.
    Stitch across the lower edge of the front facings,
    allowing a 1in (2.5cm) hem. Cut diagonally across
    the corners, taking care not to cut into the stitching.

9   Turn the facings right side out and press. Press the back
    facing to the inside of the garment. Pin the lower, turned
    edge of the facing to the pyjama back, then tack and
    stitch in place in between the shoulder seams, either
    by hand or by machine.

Pocket

10 With right sides together, pin and stitch around
    the pocket, leaving an opening of around 2in (5cm).
    Trim the seam and cut diagonally across the corners,
    taking care not to cut the stitching. Turn the pocket
    right side out and press well. Slipstitch the opening
    closed *(see page 151)*.

11 Pin the pocket to the outside of the left front, matching
    the small dots. Topstitch close to the side and lower
    edges *(see page 151)*.

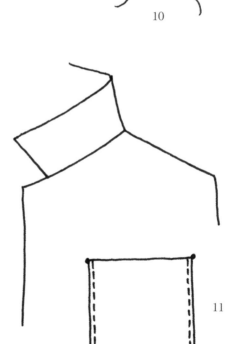

11

12

Sleeves and side seams

12 Run two rows of gathering stitches *(see page 156)* in between the notches, by hand or using a long machine stitch, working one row along the seam line and the other ¼in (6mm) inside the seam line, to ease the fullness of the top of the sleeve.

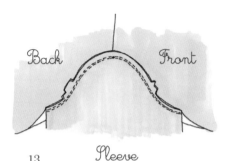

Back *Front*

Sleeve

13

13 With right sides together, pin the sleeve to the armhole, aligning the centre dot with the shoulder seam. Match notches and seam lines at the underarms. Pull up the gathering stitches to fit, adjusting them so they are evenly distributed. Insert plenty of pins to help ease the fullness of the sleeve head. Stitch between the underarm seams and work a second line of stitches close to the first for added strength. Trim each side of the seam allowance separately, from the underarm to the notch. Press the seam towards the sleeve.

14 Stitch the sleeve and side seams, matching notches and underarm seams.

Hems

15 Turn up the sleeve hems and press. Turn under and press ¼in (6mm) on the lower edge of the sleeve. Stitch close to the turned raw edges.

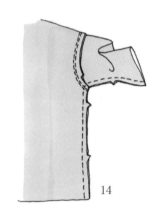

14

16 Turn up the shirt hem and press. Turn under and press ¼in (6mm) on the hem, tucking it under behind the front facings. Stitch close to the turned raw edge, working right across the front facings to the end.

Finishing off

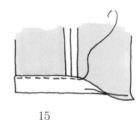

15

17 Finish by working four ⅞in (2.25cm) vertical buttonholes by hand or machine *(see page 163)* on the right front for a girl and left front for a boy, to correspond with the position of the buttons, indicated on the pattern by an 'X'. The shank of the button should be situated in the centre of the vertical buttonhole. Attach the buttons to the left front for a girl and right front for a boy.

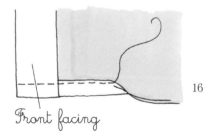

Front facing

16

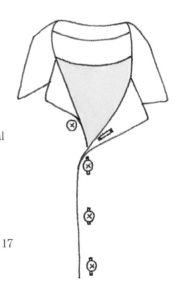

17

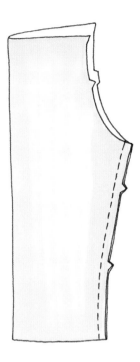

1

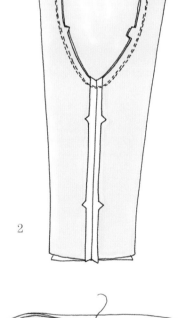

2

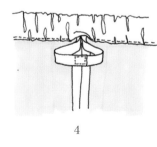

3

Pyjama trousers

Trouser legs

1   With right sides together, matching the notches, stitch the inside leg seams.

2   With right sides together, matching the notches at the front and back, slip one leg inside the other. Pin and stitch from the front waist, across the leg seams and up to the back waist. It is a good idea to work a second row of stitches close to the first on this seam for added strength. Turn the trousers right side out.

Waistband

3   Turn and press the top edge of the trousers to the inside along the fold line. Press under ¼in (6mm) along the raw edge. Sew in place, close to the turned raw edge, leaving an opening at the back of 1in (2.5cm).

4   Using a bodkin or a safety pin, insert the elastic through the opening in the waistband. Make sure the elastic does not twist as you pass it through the waistband and back out of the opening. Overlap ¾in (2cm) at the ends of the elastic so it lays flat. Stitch the ends together securely by hand or machine.

5   Push the ends of the elastic into the waistband and stitch the opening to close.

Trouser hem

6   Turn under 1in (2.5cm) at the hem of each leg and press. Turn the raw edge under and press, then stitch the hem.

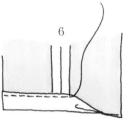

4

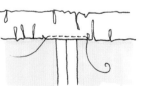

5

6

shirt

This smart shirt has a one-piece collar, shaped hem and long sleeves with buttoned cuffs. For a more casual look, the shirt can be made with short sleeves.

The following guide shows how much material you will need for an average-sized child.

FABRIC WIDTH (WITHOUT NAP)	1 YEAR OLD	2 YEAR OLD	3 YEAR OLD
36in (90cm)	Long sleeves: 1¼yd (1.1m) Short sleeves: 1⅛yd (1m)	Long sleeves: 1¼yd (1.1m) Short sleeves: 1⅛yd (1m)	Long sleeves: 1⅓yd (1.2m) Short sleeves: 1⅛yd (1m)
45in (115cm)	Long sleeves: 1yd (0.9m) Short sleeves: ⅞yd (0.8m)	Long sleeves: 1yd (0.9m) Short sleeves: ⅞yd (0.8m)	Long sleeves: 1yd (0.9m) Short sleeves: ⅞yd (0.8m)
60in (150cm)	Long sleeves: ¾yd (0.7m) Short sleeves: ⅔yd (0.6m)	Long sleeves: ¾yd (0.7m) Short sleeves: ⅔yd (0.6m)	Long sleeves: ⅞yd (0.8m) Short sleeves: ¾yd (0.7m)
36in (90cm)-wide lightweight iron-on interfacing	½yd (0.45m)	⅔yd (0.6m)	⅔yd (0.6m)

Suggested fabrics
Cotton shirting, lawn, poplin, linen, chambray, needlecord

Sewing notions
- Thread to match fabric
- Long-sleeved shirt: 8 x ½in (1.25cm) buttons
- Short-sleeved shirt: 6 x ½in (1.25cm) buttons

Seam allowances
Take ⅝in (1.5cm) seam allowances throughout, unless otherwise stated.

Finished measurements
Back length:
1 year: 16⅓in (41.5cm)
2 years: 17⅓in (44cm)
3 years: 18⅓in (46.5cm)

36in (90cm) wide – SHORT SLEEVE
SELVEDGES

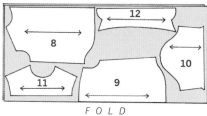

FOLD

45in (115cm) wide – SHORT SLEEVE
SELVEDGES

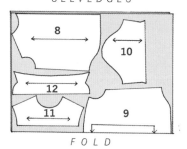

FOLD

Pattern pieces on sheets C and D
8   Front (cut 2 in main fabric and 2 front facings in interfacing)
9   Back (cut 1 in main fabric)
10 Sleeve (cut 2 in main fabric)
11 Yoke (cut 2 in main fabric)
12 Collar (cut 2 in main fabric and 1 in interfacing)
13 Cuff (cut 2 in main fabric and 2 in interfacing

36in (90cm) wide – LONG SLEEVE
SELVEDGES

FOLD

45in (115cm) wide – LONG SLEEVE

SELVEDGES

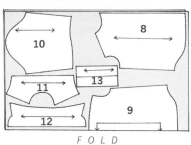

10

8

13

11

9

12

FOLD

60in (150cm) wide – SHORT & LONG SLEEVE

SELVEDGES

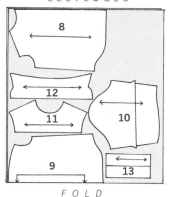

8

12

11

10

9

13

FOLD

Omit cuff for short-sleeved shirt

Instructions

1   Staystitch *(see page 151)* the neck edges of the front and yoke pieces to prevent the fabric from stretching.

Join yoke, front and back

2   With right sides together, pin one yoke piece to the back of the shirt. Place the right side of the remaining yoke piece to the wrong side of the back of the shirt. This will be the yoke facing. Stitch through all layers, easing the back to fit between the notches. Press the yoke facing up.

3   With the right side of the yoke facing to the wrong side of the front pieces, stitch together, matching notches. Press the seams towards the yoke facing.

4   Press under ⅝in (1.5cm) on the front edges of the yoke then press the yoke up. On the outside of the garment, pin the pressed edges of the yoke over the seams. Topstitch *(see page 151)* close to the pressed edges.

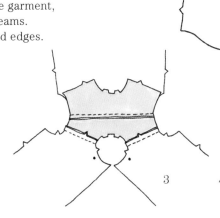

1

Yoke facing

Yoke

Back

2

3

4

Key

 Right side of fabric

Wrong side of fabric

 Interfacing

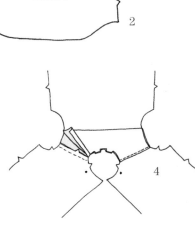

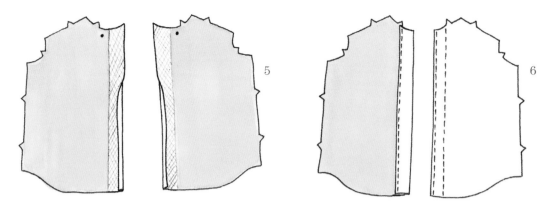

5

6

Facings

5   Following the manufacturer's instructions, apply iron-on interfacing *(see page 145)* to the wrong side of the left and right front facings to the fold line. Turn under and press ¼in (6mm) along the outside edge of the front facings.

6   Press the facings to the inside along the fold line. Pin and stitch the facings down, close to the turned edge. Topstitch close to the front edges of the shirt.

Collar

7   Following the manufacturer's instructions, apply iron-on interfacing to the wrong side of one collar piece. This will be the under collar. Press under ⅝in (1.5cm) on neck edge of the under collar. Trim to ¼in (6mm).

8   The second collar piece will be the top collar. With right sides together, pin the top collar to the under collar. Stitch around the three outer edges, leaving the neck edge open. Trim the seams and notch the curves. Cut diagonally across the corners and snip into the inverted corners *(see page 153)*.

9   Turn the collar right side out and press. With the right side of the top collar to the right side of the yoke facing, matching notches and dots, pin and stitch the top collar to the neck edge, sewing through all layers. Trim and snip the seam at the neck edge. Press the seam towards the collar.

10 On the outside of the garment, pin the pressed edge of the under collar over the seam, matching the dots. Topstitch close to the pressed edge. Topstitch close to the edge of the collar, starting and ending at the neck edge.

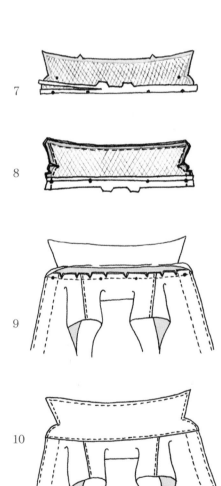

7

8

9

10

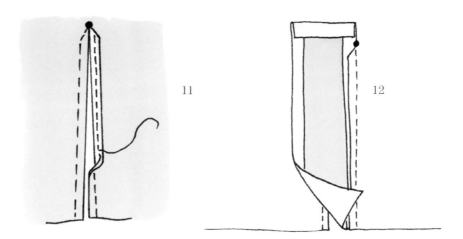

11   12

Long sleeves only

11 Staystitch the sleeve along the broken line indicated on the pattern. Slash between the stitching to the small dot. Turn under a narrow hem at the back edge of the sleeve opening along the staystitching line and sew down.

12 Cut two straight strips of fabric, each measuring 2in (5cm) wide by 3½in (9cm) long. With the right side of the strip to the wrong side of the sleeve, pin and sew the strip to the staystitching on the front side of the sleeve opening, taking a ¼in (6mm) seam on the strip. Press the seam towards the strip. Turn under and press ¼in (6mm) on the side and top edges of the strip.

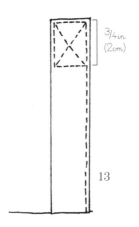

¾in (2cm)

13

13 On the right side of the sleeve, pin the pressed edge of the strip over the seam. Stitch close to the pressed edge. Stitch the top of the strip to the sleeve, forming a rectangle ¾in (2cm) deep. Stitch diagonally across the rectangle to reinforce the top of the opening.

14 Make pleats in the sleeve by folding along the solid lines on the pattern, with right sides together, matching the broken lines. Tack along the broken lines. Lay the pleats away from the opening.

14

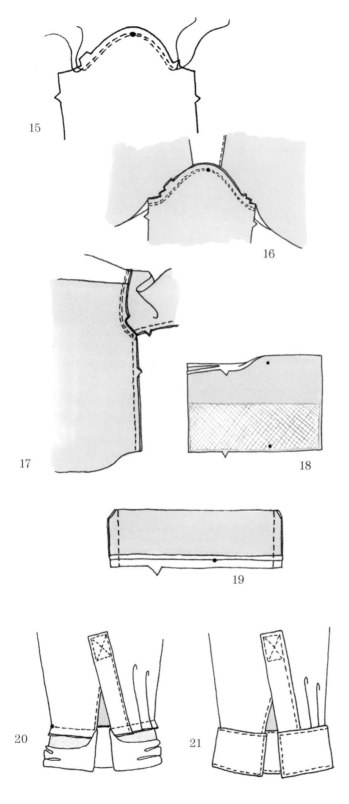

Sleeves and side seams

15 Run two rows of gathering stitches *(see page 156)* in between the notches, by hand or using a long machine stitch, working one row along the seam line and the other ¼in (6mm) inside the seam line, to ease the fullness of the top of the sleeve.

16 With right sides together, pin the sleeve to the armhole, aligning the centre dot on the sleeve with the dot on the armhole edge of the yoke. Match notches and seam lines at the underarms. Pull up the gathering stitches to fit, adjusting them so they are evenly distributed. Insert plenty of pins to help ease the fullness of the sleeve head. Stitch between the underarm seams and work a second line of stitches close to the first for added strength. Trim each side of the seam allowance separately, from the underarm to the notch. Press the seam towards the sleeve.

17 Stitch the sleeve and side seams, matching notches and underarm seams.

Cuffs (long sleeves only)

18 Following the manufacturer's instructions, apply iron-on interfacing *(see page 145)* to the wrong side of the cuffs to the fold line. Press under ⅝in (1.5cm) along the long edge of the side of the cuff without interfacing. Trim to ¼in (6mm).

19 With right sides together, turn the cuff along the fold line, pin and stitch the short edges. Trim the seams and cut diagonally across the corners. Turn right side out and press.

20 With right side of the interfaced side of the cuff to the wrong side of the sleeve, pin and stitch together, matching the notches and the small dot to the sleeve seam. Trim and press the seam towards the interfaced side of the cuff.

21 On the outside of the sleeve, pin the pressed edge of the cuff over the seam. Stitch close to the pressed edge. Topstitch close to the outer edges of the cuff. Remove the tacking stitches.

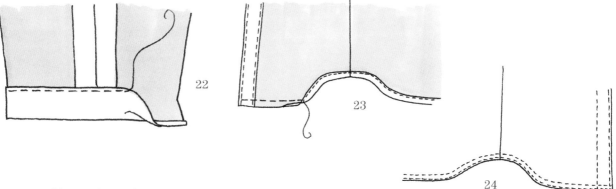

Sleeve hem (short sleeves only)

22 Turn up the sleeve hems and press. Turn under and press ¼in (6mm) on the lower edge of the sleeve. Stitch close to the turned raw edges.

Hem

23 Staystitch along the ⅝in (1.5cm) seam line at the lower edge. Turn the raw edge to the inside along the staystitching. Turn under the raw edge and press. Stitch in place.

24 Topstitch close to the outer edge of the hem.

Finishing off

25 Finish by working buttonholes by hand or machine *(see page 163)* on the right front for a girl and left front for a boy. Make a horizontal buttonhole on the collar, as indicated on the pattern. Make five ⅝in (1.5cm) vertical buttonholes down the front of the shirt to correspond with the position of the buttons, indicated on the pattern by an 'X'. The shank of the button should be situated in the centre of the vertical buttonhole. Attach the buttons to the left front for a girl and right front for a boy *(see page 165)*. On the long-sleeved shirt, work buttonholes in the cuffs by hand or machine, as indicated on the pattern. Mark the position of buttons on the cuffs to correspond with the buttonholes. Attach the buttons to the cuffs.

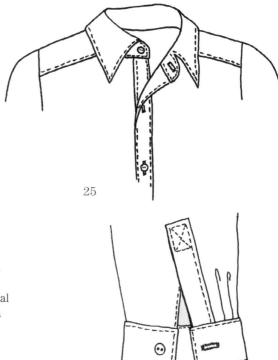

romper

This cute romper has front-buttoned shoulder straps crossed at the back, an elasticated back waist, and snap fasteners at the inside leg for easy nappy changes.

The following guide shows how much material you will need for an average-sized child.

FABRIC WIDTH (WITHOUT NAP)	6 MONTHS	1 YEAR OLD	2 YEAR OLD
36in (90cm)	**Girl's romper** Main fabric: 1³⁄₈yd (1.3m) Facing: ¹⁄₂yd (0.45m) **Boy's romper** Main fabric: 1¹⁄₄yd (1.1m) Facing: ¹⁄₂yd (0.45m)	**Girl's romper** Main fabric: 1¹⁄₂yd (1.4m) Facing: ¹⁄₂yd (0.45m) **Boy's romper** Main fabric: 1¹⁄₄yd (1.1m) Facing: ¹⁄₂yd (0.45m)	**Girl's romper** Main fabric: 1¹⁄₂yd (1.4m) Facing: ¹⁄₂yd (0.45m) **Boy's romper** Main fabric: 1¹⁄₃yd (1.2m) Facing: ¹⁄₂yd (0.45m)
45in (115cm)	**Girl's romper** Main fabric: 1¹⁄₄yd (1.1m) Facing: ¹⁄₂yd (0.45m) **Boy's romper** Main fabric: 1yd (0.9m) Facing: ¹⁄₂yd (0.45m)	**Girl's romper** Main fabric: 1¹⁄₄yd (1.1m) Facing: ¹⁄₂yd (0.45m) **Boy's romper** Main fabric: 1yd (0.9m) Facing: ¹⁄₂yd (0.45m)	**Girl's romper** Main fabric: 1¹⁄₃yd (1.2m) Facing: ¹⁄₂yd (0.45m) **Boy's romper** Main fabric: 1¹⁄₈yd (1m) Facing: ¹⁄₂yd (0.45m)
60in (150cm)	**Girl's romper** Main fabric: 1yd (0.9m) Facing: ¹⁄₂yd (0.45m) **Boy's romper** Main fabric: ⁷⁄₈yd (0.8m) Facing: ¹⁄₂yd (0.45m)	**Girl's romper** Main fabric: 1yd (0.9m) Facing: ¹⁄₂yd (0.45m) **Boy's romper** Main fabric: ⁷⁄₈yd (0.8m) Facing: ¹⁄₂yd (0.45m)	**Girl's romper** Main fabric: 1¹⁄₈yd (1m) Facing: ¹⁄₂yd (0.45m) **Boy's romper** Main fabric: 1yd (0.9m) Facing: ¹⁄₂yd (0.45m)

Suggested fabrics

Main fabric: Light- to medium-weight fabrics, shirting, poplin, seersucker, gingham, fine needlecord, lightweight denim

Facing: Cotton, cotton mix

Sewing notions

- Thread to match fabric
- 1in (2.5cm)-wide elastic to fit the back of the waist comfortably, with an extra ³⁄₄in (2cm)
- 2 lengths of ¹⁄₄in (6mm)-wide elastic to fit around the leg comfortably with an extra 2in (5cm)
- Bodkin or safety pin
- 3 x ³⁄₈in (1cm) snap fasteners
- 4 x ⁵⁄₈in (1.5cm) buttons

Seam allowances

Take ⅝in (1.5cm) seam allowances throughout, unless otherwise stated.

Pattern pieces on sheets D and E

14 Skirt (cut 2 in main fabric)
15 Shorts back (cut 2 in main fabric)
16 Shorts front (cut 2 in main fabric)
17 Shoulder strap
   (cut 2 in main fabric)
18 Bib (cut 1 in main fabric,
   cut 1 in facing fabric)
19 Waist casing (cut 1 in main fabric,
   cut 1 in facing fabric)

Finished measurements

Length from waist at side seam:
6 months: 10in (26cm)
1 year: 10½in (27cm)
2 years: 11in (28cm)

Broken lines indicate reverse side of patterns

36in (90cm) wide – GIRL'S ROMPER

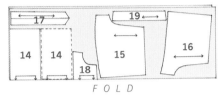

36in (90cm) wide – BOY'S ROMPER

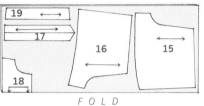

36in (90cm), 45in (115cm) and 60in (150cm) wide – FACING

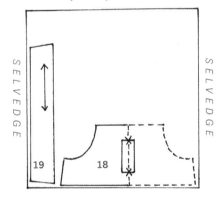

Open fabric out to cut waist casing

45in (115cm) wide – GIRL'S ROMPER

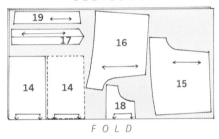

45in (115cm) wide – BOY'S ROMPER

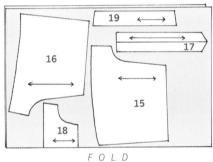

60in (150cm) wide – GIRL'S ROMPER

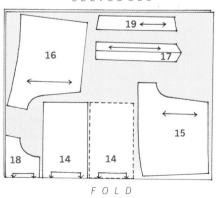

60in (150cm) wide – BOY'S ROMPER

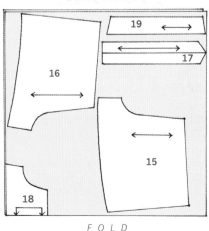

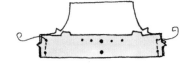

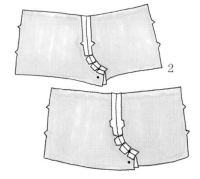

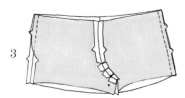

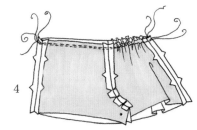

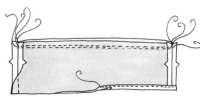

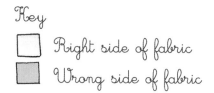

Instructions

Facings

1   With right sides together and notches matching, stitch the bib facing and waist-casing facing together up to the small dot at the top edge. Press seams open.

Shorts

2   Join the centre-front and centre-back seams. Stitch a second row over the first to reinforce the seam. Clip the curves *(see page 153)* and press seams open.

3   With right sides together, stitch side seams of shorts. Trim seams and press open.

4   Run two rows of gathering stitches *(see page 156)* along the upper edge of the front and back of the shorts, by hand or using a long machine stitch, working one row along the seam line and the other ¼in (6mm) inside the seam line. Pull up the gathering stitches on the front and back of the shorts separately to fit the lower edge of the bib and waist-casing facings, matching the seams.

Skirt (optional)

5   With right sides together, stitch side seams of skirt. Trim seams and press open. Turn under and press ⅝in (1.5cm) on the hem of the skirt. Turn under the raw edge, press and stitch. Gather the skirt as for the shorts in Step 4.

6   Place the wrong side of the skirt over the right side of the shorts, matching the side seams. Adjust the gathers to fit and tack together at the top edge.

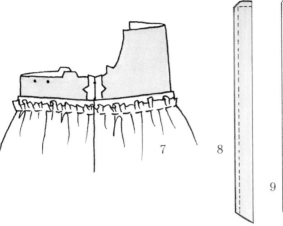

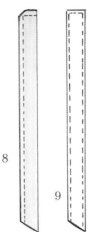

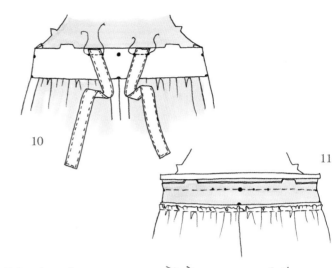

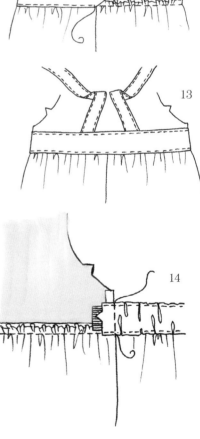

Attach shorts (and skirt) to facing

7   With right side of bib and waist-casing facing to wrong side of the gathered edge of the shorts, matching the side seams and the large dot to the centre-back seam, pin and stitch together. Trim and layer the seam if necessary to reduce bulk *(see page 153)*. Press the seam towards the facings. Remove tacking stitches.

Shoulder straps

8   With right sides together, fold the strap along the line indicated on the pattern. Stitch along the edges, leaving the slanted end open. Trim the seam and cut diagonally into the corners, taking care not to cut into the stitching.

9   Turn the strap right-side out and press. Topstitch *(see page 151)* close to the edges of the strap.

10   On the right side of the waist-casing facing, matching the dots, tack the straps in position with the seams facing towards the centre, aligning the raw edges with the top edge of the waist-casing facing.

Waist casing

11   Press under ⅝in (1.5cm) on the lower edge of the waist casing. With right sides together, matching notches and the small dots to the side seams, stitch the waist casing to the waist-casing facing at the top edge between the small dots, sandwiching the straps between them. Press waist casing up. Press seam towards waist casing.

12   On the outside of the garment, pin the pressed edge of the waist casing over the seam, matching the small dots with the side seam. Topstitch close to the pressed edge between the small dots.

13   Topstitch close to the top edge of the waist casing between the small dots.

14   Use a bodkin or safety pin to thread the elastic through the opening at the waist casing. Adjust to fit, trim the excess elastic and stitch down at the side seams to secure the ends.

15

Bib

15 Turn under and press ⅝in (1.5cm) at side seams and lower edge of bib.

16 With right sides of bib and bib facing together, pin and stitch the armhole and top edges together, leaving the side and lower edges open. Trim seams, snip curves and cut diagonally into the corners, taking care not to cut into the stitching.

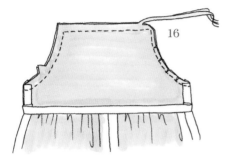

16

17 On the outside of the garment, pin the pressed lower edge of the bib over the seam. Topstitch close to the pressed edge.

18 Topstitch the pressed side edges down over the waist casing. Then topstitch close to the armhole and top edges of the bib.

Leg casings and elastic

19 Turn under and press ¾in (2cm) on the hem of the leg edges. Turn under the raw edge, press and stitch to form a casing. Topstitch close to the outer edge of the casing.

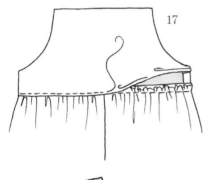

17

20 Using a bodkin or a safety pin, insert the elastic through the opening in the leg casing. Adjust to fit and stitch across the ends.

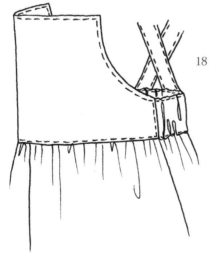

18

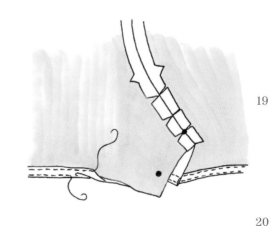

19

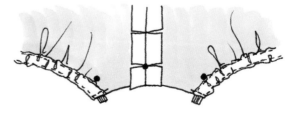

20

Inside-leg fastening

21 Cut two 1⅛in (3cm)-wide bias strips *(see page 160)* to fit the length of each inner-leg edge at the front and back, allowing an extra ¾in (2cm) on the length of each strip. With right sides together, pin a bias strip to the inner leg edge of the front and the back, turning under ⅜in (1cm) of the strip at each end. Stitch in place, allowing a ¼in (6mm) seam.

22 Press the seam towards the binding and press the bias strip to the inside. Turn under the raw edge and stitch. Slipstitch *(see page 151)* the ends of the bias strips to the edge of the hem.

Finishing off

23 Sew snap fasteners to the front and back inside legs *(see page 165)* at the medium dots.

24 Work buttonholes by hand or machine in the front. Sew two buttons securely *(see page 165)* to each strap, indicated on the pattern by an 'X'.

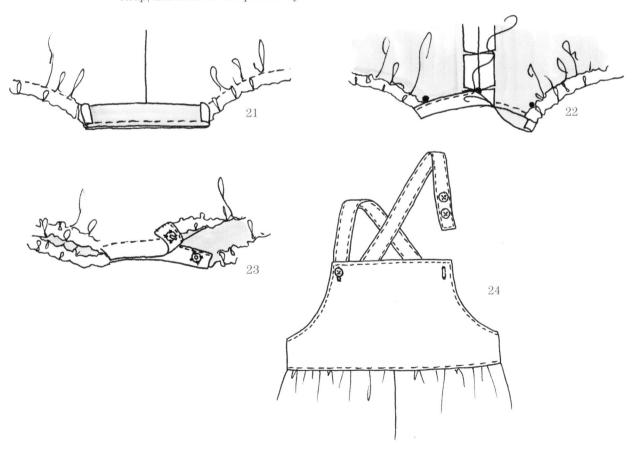

coat

This smart little coat will equally suit a boy or a girl. It is fully lined, has useful front flap pockets, a Peter-Pan collar and an optional inside welt pocket.

The following guide shows how much material you will need for an average-sized child.

FABRIC WIDTH (WITHOUT NAP)	1 YEAR OLD	2 YEAR OLD	3 YEAR OLD
36in (90cm)	Main fabric: 1½yd (1.4m) Lining fabric: 1yd (0.9m)	Main fabric: 1⅝yd (1.5m) Lining fabric: 1yd (0.9m)	Main fabric: 1⅝yd (1.5m) Lining fabric: 1⅛yd (1m)
45in (115cm)	Main fabric: 1¼yd (1.1m) Lining fabric: ⅞yd (0.8m)	Main fabric: 1⅓yd (1.2m) Lining fabric: 1yd (0.9m)	Main fabric: 1⅓yd (1.2m) Lining fabric: 1yd (0.9m)
60in (150cm)	Main fabric: 1yd (0.9m) Lining fabric: ⅔yd (0.6m)	Main fabric: 1⅛yd (1m) Lining fabric: ⅔yd (0.6m)	Main fabric: 1⅛yd (1m) Lining fabric: ⅔yd (0.6m)
36in (90cm)-wide iron-on woven interfacing	⅔yd (0.6m)	⅔yd (0.6m)	⅔yd (0.6m)

Suggested fabrics

Wool, tweed, needlecord, corduroy, linen
For lining: cotton, cotton mix
Not suitable for obvious diagonal prints

Sewing notions

- Thread to match fabric
- 3 x ⅞in (2.25cm) buttons
- 1 x ⅜in (1cm) snap fastening

Seam allowances

Take ⅝in (1.5cm) seam allowances throughout, unless otherwise stated.

Finished measurements

Back length:
1 year: 17½in (44.5cm)
2 years: 18½in (47cm)
3 years: 19½in (49.5cm)

36in (90cm) wide – MAIN FABRIC

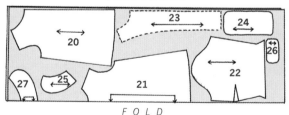

36in (90cm) wide – LINING FABRIC

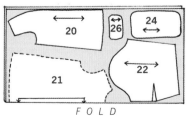

Open fabric out to cut inside pocket

45in (115cm) wide – MAIN FABRIC

SELVEDGES

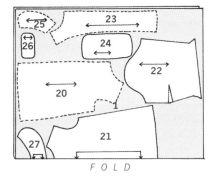

FOLD

45in (115cm) wide – LINING FABRIC

SELVEDGES

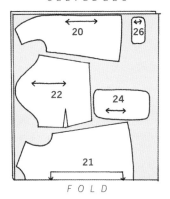

FOLD

Open fabric out to cut inside pocket

Broken lines indicate reverse side of pattern

60in (150cm) wide – MAIN FABRIC

SELVEDGES

FOLD

60in (150cm) wide – LINING FABRIC

SELVEDGES

FOLD

Key

☐ Right side of fabric

▨ Wrong side of fabric

▩ Interfacing

Pattern pieces on sheets E and F

20 Front (cut 2 in main fabric, cut 2 in lining fabric)

21 Back (cut 1 in main fabric, cut 1 in lining fabric)

22 Sleeve (cut 2 in main fabric, cut 2 in lining fabric)

23 Front facing (cut 2 in main fabric, cut 2 in interfacing)

24 Pocket (cut 2 in main fabric and for optional inside pocket cut 1 in lining fabric)

25 Under collar (cut 2 in main fabric, cut 2 in interfacing)

26 Pocket flap (cut 2 in main fabric, cut 2 in lining fabric, cut 2 in interfacing)

27 Top collar (cut 1 in main fabric)

Instructions

1 Staystitch *(see page 151)* the neck edges of the front and back pieces and the front facings to prevent the fabric from stretching.

Bound buttonholes

Work bound buttonholes *(see page 164)*, on right front for girl and left front for boy. Hand-worked or machine buttonholes are added at the end, after making up the coat.

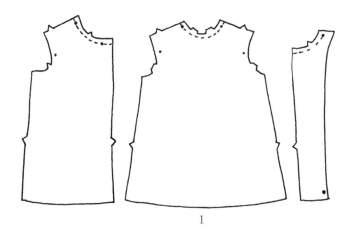

1

Pockets

2   Following the manufacturer's instructions, apply iron-on interfacing *(see page 145)* to the wrong side of the two pocket-flap lining pieces. With right sides together, stitch the pocket-flap linings to the main fabric pieces around the outer edges. Trim the seams and notch the curves *(see page 153)*.

3   Turn right side out and press. Tack the raw edges together. With the right side of pocket flap to the right side of coat front, tack the flap in position between the dots as indicated on the pattern piece, allowing a ¼in (6mm) seam.

4   With right sides together, matching the corresponding markings, stitch the pocket to the coat front on the seam line around the slash. The ends of the lower line taper slightly, so they will not show when the flap is pressed down. Slash the pocket and front on the line indicated on the pattern to within ½in (1.25cm) of both ends. Snip diagonally into the corners, taking care not to go through the stitches.

5   Draw the pocket through the slash to the wrong side of the garment. Fold and press the lower section of the pocket to form a binding at the lower edge of the opening on the right side. The binding can be slipstitched to each side of the opening, if you wish, to prevent it from moving when completing the pocket.

6   On the wrong side of the coat, with right sides together, press the upper section of the pocket over the lower section. Stitch the outer edges of the pocket together, catching the triangular pieces down in the stitching. Press the pocket flap down.

Join back to front

7   With right sides together, matching notches and dots, pin and stitch the front pieces to the back piece at the shoulder seams, easing *(see page 152)* the back to fit the front. Press seams open.

Collar

8 Following the manufacturer's instructions, apply iron-on interfacing to the wrong side of the under-collar pieces. With right sides together, matching notches, pin and stitch the under-collar pieces together at the centre back. Press the seam open.

9 To ease in the fullness of the top collar, use a long machine stitch to work a line of stitching along the seam line of the outside edge.

10 With right sides together, matching notches and the medium dots at the centre front, pin the top collar to the under collar. Ease the top collar to fit by pulling the machine stitching. Stitch around the outer edges, leaving the neck edge open. Trim the seams and notch the curves.

11 Turn right side out and press, rolling the seam towards the under collar and aligning the raw edges. Tack the raw edges of the collar together.

12 With the right side of the under collar to the right side of the coat, pin and tack the collar to the neck edge, matching the notches and the small dots to the shoulder seams.

Sleeves and side seams

13 Stitch the dart in the sleeve and press down. On heavy-weight fabric, the dart can be slashed to within ½in (1.25cm) of the point and pressed open to reduce bulk *(see page 155)*. Run two rows of gathering stitches *(see page 156)* in between the notches, by hand or using a long machine stitch, working one row along the seam line and the other ¼in (6mm) inside the seam line, to ease the fullness of the top of the sleeve.

14 With right sides together, pin the sleeve to the armhole, aligning the centre dot with the shoulder. Match notches, dots and seam lines at the underarms. Pull up the gathering stitches to fit. Tack the sleeve in place, easing in the fullness. Stitch between the underarm seams, then work a second line of stitches close to the first for added strength. Trim each side of the seam allowance separately, from the underarm to the notch. Press the seam towards the sleeve.

15 Stitch the sleeve and side seams, matching notches and underarm seams. Press seams open.

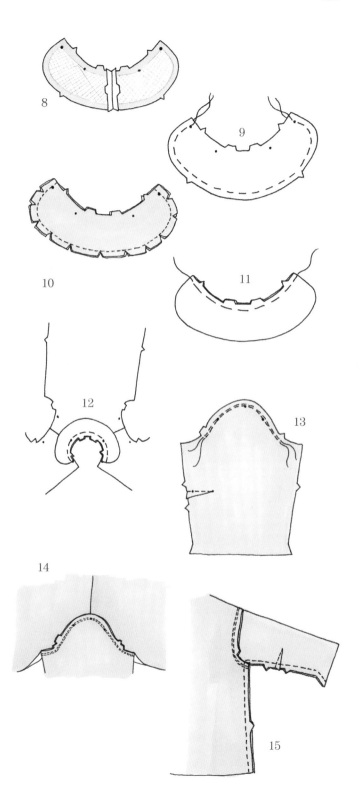

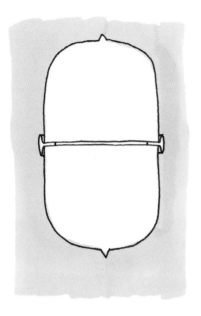

16

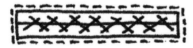

17

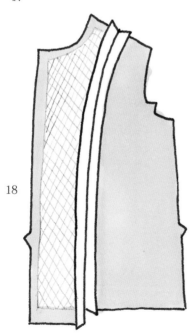

18

Lining and facings

16 If you do not wish to insert an inside pocket, skip to Step 18. For the optional lining pocket, position the pocket piece on the inside of the right or left front lining piece. Follow Step 4 to attach the pocket to the lining with the shorter pocket section below the opening. The inside pocket is square and not tapered like the front pockets. Draw the pocket through the slash to the wrong side of the lining. Fold and press the edges to meet in the centre of the opening, forming an even binding on each side.

17 On the right side, catch stitch *(see page 150)* the edges of the opening together. Stitch around the opening, close to the seam line, to secure the binding. On the wrong side of the lining, stitch the outer edges of the pocket together as in Step 6. Remove catch stitching and press.

18 Following the manufacturer's instructions, apply iron-on interfacing to the wrong side of the left and right front facings. With right sides together, pin and stitch the front linings to the front facings, matching the small dot with the edge of the lining and stopping within ¾in (2cm) of the raw edge of the lining. With right sides together, matching notches, pin and stitch the lining front pieces to the lining back at the shoulder seams. Press the seams open. Follow Steps 13–15 to complete the sleeves and side seams.

19 With right sides of coat and lining together, matching the seams and pattern markings, pin and stitch the front and neck edges together, leaving the hem loose. Trim the seam, clip the curves and cut diagonally across the corners, taking care not to go through the stitches.

19

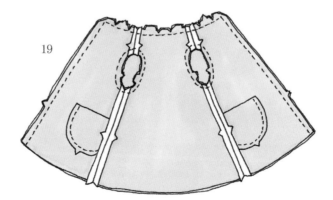

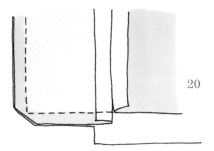

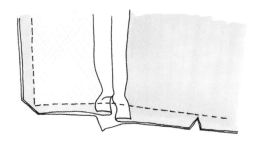

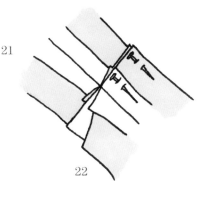

Hem

20 With right sides together, stitch across the lower edges
of the front facings allowing a 1in (2.5cm) hem. Trim the
seam and cut diagonally across the corners, taking care
not to cut into the stitching.

21 With right sides together, align the lower edge of the
lining with the edge of the coat. Pin and stitch in place
along the seam line. Trim the seam and notch the curve.

22 Turn up around 2in (5cm) on the hem of the sleeve
lining and, with right sides together, insert it into the
sleeve, matching the seams. Make sure that neither the
sleeve nor lining are twisted. Pin and stitch the sleeve
and lining together. Repeat for the other sleeve.

23 To turn the work right side out, carefully unpick around
4–6in (10–15cm) on the seam of the sleeve lining. This
will provide you with a pressed seam, making it easier to
stitch closed. Pull the coat to the right side through the
opening in the sleeve lining. To close the opening in the
sleeve lining, with wrong sides together, pin and stitch
close to the pressed edges on the right side. Take care
not to catch the main sleeve fabric in the stitches.

24 On the inside of the coat, slipstitch the opening at the
edge where the facing and hem meet. On the right side
of the coat, run a line of stitches by hand or machine
along the shoulder seam, from the neck edge to the end
of the front facing, to catch the lining down.

25 Finish by working buttonholes by hand or machine
(see page 163) on the right front for a girl and left
front for a boy, as indicated on the pattern. If bound
buttonholes were made, hem the facings around them
(see page 164). Overlap the fronts of the coat, matching
the centre front. Mark the position of buttons to
correspond with the buttonholes. Attach the buttons to
the left front for a girl and right front for a boy (see page
165). Sew the snap fastening to the coat front at the
neck edge to hold the corner in place under the collar
(see page 165).

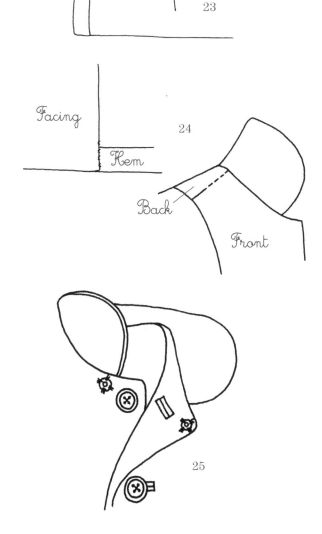

sun dress

This simple sun dress has a keyhole neckline with a button-and-loop fastening at the back. It can also be worn over a long-sleeved top during the cooler months.

The following guide shows how much material you will need for an average-sized child.

FABRIC WIDTH (WITHOUT NAP)	1 YEAR OLD	2 YEAR OLD	3 YEAR OLD
36in (90cm)	Main fabric: 1yd (0.9m)	Main fabric: 1yd (0.9m)	Main fabric: 1yd (0.9m)
45in (115cm)	Main fabric: ⅔ (0.6m)	Main fabric: ⅔yd (0.6m)	Main fabric: ¾yd (0.7m)
60in (150cm)	Main fabric: ⅔ yd (0.6m)	Main fabric: ⅔ yd (0.6m)	Main fabric: ¾yd (0.7m)

Suggested fabrics
Linen, lawn, chambray, poplin, shirting, voile

For the binding
Contrast fabric: ½ x ½yd (0.45 x 0.45m)

Sewing notions
- Thread to match fabric
- 1 x ⅝in (1.5cm) button
- Large needle
- Strong thread, such as buttonhole thread

Pattern pieces on sheet A
28 Front (cut 1 in main fabric)
29 Back (cut 2 in main fabric)

Seam allowances
Take ⅝in (1.5cm) seam allowances on side and shoulder seams and ⅜in (1cm) on bound edges.

Finished measurements
Back length:
1 year: 19¼in (49cm)
2 years: 20¼in (51.5cm)
3 years: 21¼in (54cm)

36in (90cm) wide

SELVEDGES

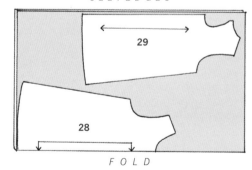

FOLD

45in (115cm) and 60in (150cm) wide

SELVEDGES

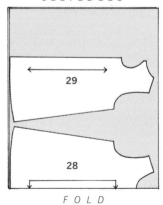

FOLD

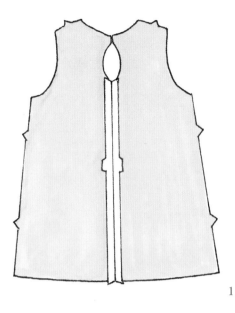

1

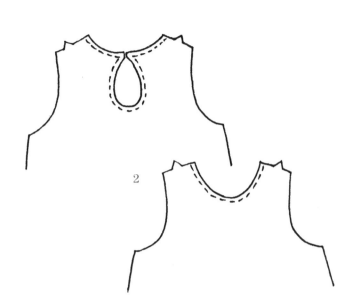

2

Instructions

Join back seam

1   With right sides together, stitch the back seam up to the keyhole opening. Press seam open.

2   Staystitch *(see page 151)* the keyhole opening and neck edges of the back and front at the ⅜in (1cm) seam allowance.

Join front to back

3   With right sides together, stitch the front to the back at the shoulders and side seams. Press seams open.

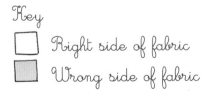

Key

☐ *Right side of fabric*

▨ *Wrong side of fabric*

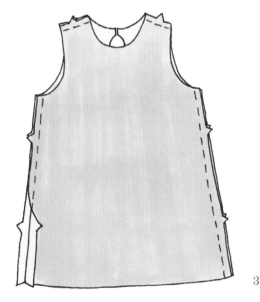

3

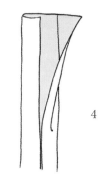

Binding

4   Cut 1½in (4cm)-wide bias strips from the contrast
fabric and sew the short edges together to make the
binding *(see page 160)*. Using all of the contrast fabric
will make approximately 4yd (3.7m) of binding, but the
sun dress will use only around 2yd (1.8m). Press a ⅜in
(1cm) seam allowance along each long edge.

5   To bind the keyhole opening, open out one pressed
edge of the binding. With the right side of the binding
to the inside of the back of the dress, pin the creased
edge of the binding to the ⅜in (1cm) seam allowance
around the keyhole opening. Stitch in place.

6   Turn the binding over the seam allowances to the right
side of the garment and pin the pressed edges over the
seams. Topstitch *(see page 151)* close to the pressed
edges. Press the bound edges. Trim the excess binding
at each end to neaten.

7   To bind the armholes, open out one pressed edge
of the binding. Turn under ⅜in (1cm) at the short
end and, with the right side of the binding to the
inside of the garment, align the turned edge with the
underarm seam. Pin and stitch the creased edge of
the binding to the ⅜in (1cm) seam allowance of the
armhole, overlapping the binding at the end before
cutting away the excess.

8   Turn the binding over the seam allowances to the right
side of the garment and pin the pressed edges over the
seams. Topstitch close to the pressed edges. Press the
bound edges.

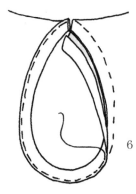

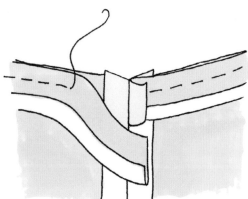

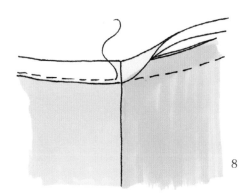

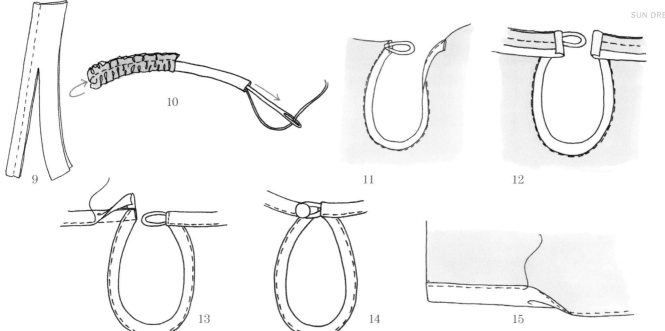

Button loop

9 Cut a 4in (10cm) length from the binding and press open. With right sides together, fold the strip in half lengthways and stitch, allowing a ⅝in (1.5cm) seam, to form a tube. Trim the seam to ⅛in (3mm).

10 To turn the tube right side out, fasten a length of strong thread to the end of the binding at the seam by sewing a few stitches over each other. Using a large needle, draw the thread through the tube, inserting the eye of the needle first. Carefully pull the fabric through to the right side. Remove the strong thread and trim the tube to 2½in (6.5cm).

11 Fold the button loop in half and overlap the ends. On the inside of the dress, position the button loop at the neck edge of the right back of the keyhole opening with the raw edges at the seam allowance. Tack in place.

Bind neck edge

12 With the right side of the binding to the inside of the garment, pin and stitch the creased edge of the binding to a ⅜in (1cm) seam allowance at the neck edge, turning under ⅜in (1cm) at each end of the binding to neaten. Press the seam towards the binding.

13 Turn the binding over the seam allowances to the right side and pin the pressed edges over the seam. Topstitch close to the pressed edge, stitching across the ends of the neck binding, encasing the ends of the button loop. Press the bound edge.

14 Stitch the button to the left back to correspond with the button loop *(see page 165)*.

Hem

15 Turn under 1in (2.5cm) at the hem and press. To ease in the fullness, stitch ¼in (6mm) from the raw edge, using a long machine stitch. Pull up the machine stitching so that the hem lies flat. Turn under the edge along the stitching and press. Stitch in place.

dungarees

These fun and practical dungarees have a simple patch pocket, shoulder straps that button up at the front and snap fastenings at the inside leg.

The following guide shows how much material you will need for an average-sized child.

FABRIC WIDTH (WITHOUT NAP)	6 MONTHS	1 YEAR OLD	2 YEAR OLD
36in (90cm)	1⅝yd (1.5m)	1¾yd (1.6m)	1¾yd (1.6m)
45in (115cm)	1⅝yd (1.5m)	1¾yd (1.6m)	1⅞yd (1.7m)
60in (150cm)	1⅓yd (1.2m)	1⅓yd (1.2m)	1⅜yd (1.3m)

Suggested fabrics

Ticking, corduroy, denim, canvas, linen, chambray

Sewing notions

- Thread to match fabric
- 4 x ⅝in (1.5cm) buttons
- 6 months: 7 x ⅜in (1cm) snap fasteners
- 1 and 2 years: 9 x ⅜in (1cm) snap fasteners

Pattern pieces
on sheets E and F

30 Front (cut 2 in main fabric)
31 Back (cut 2 in main fabric)
32 Back facing (cut 1 in main fabric)
33 Front facing (cut 1 in main fabric)
34 Shoulder strap cut 2 in main fabric)
35 Pocket (cut 2 in main fabric)

Seam allowances

Take ⅝in (1.5cm) seam allowances throughout, unless otherwise stated.

Broken lines indicate reverse side of pattern

Finished measurements

Side length of dungarees:
6 months: 15¾in (40cm)
1 year: 17⅜in (44cm)
2 years: 19in (48.5cm)

36in (90cm) wide
SELVEDGES

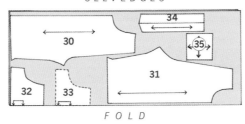

FOLD

45in (115cm) wide
SELVEDGES

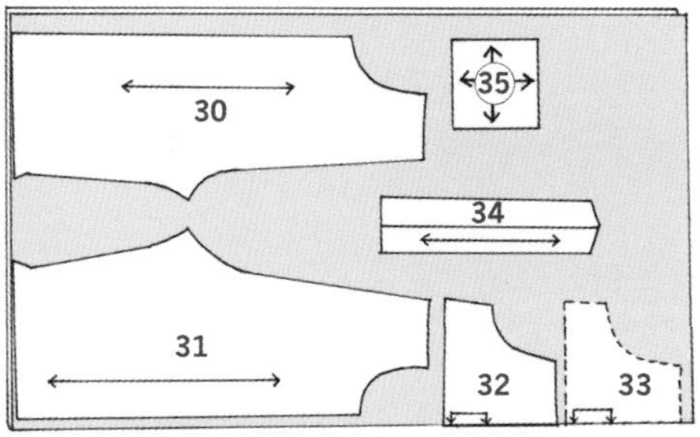

FOLD

60in (150cm) wide
SELVEDGES

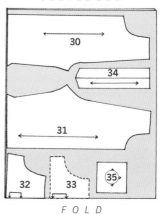

FOLD

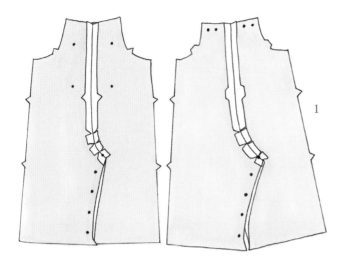

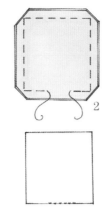

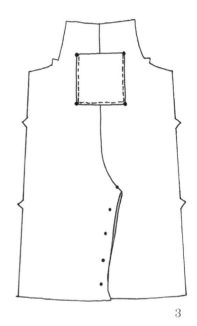

Instructions

1   Join the centre-front and centre-back seams. Stitch a second row over the first to reinforce the seam. Clip the curves *(see page 153)* and press the seams open.

Pocket

2   With right sides together, pin and stitch around the pocket, leaving an opening of around 2in (5cm). Trim the seam and cut diagonally across the corners, taking care not to cut the stitching. Turn the pocket right side out and press well. Slipstitch *(see page 151)* the opening closed.

3   On the outside of the dungarees, pin the pocket to the front, matching the small dots. Topstitch *(see page 151)* close to the side and lower edges.

Shoulder straps

4   With right sides together, fold the strap along the line indicated on the pattern. Stitch along the edges, leaving the slanted end open. Trim the seam and cut diagonally into the corners, taking care not to cut into the stitching.

5   Turn the strap right side out and press. On the outside of the dungarees, matching the dots, tack the straps in position on the back with the seams facing towards the sides, aligning the raw edges with the top edge of the back.

Key

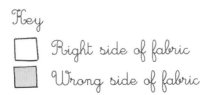

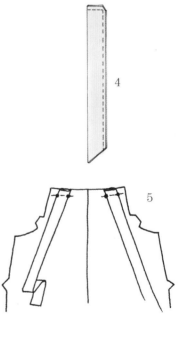

☐ *Right side of fabric*
▨ *Wrong side of fabric*

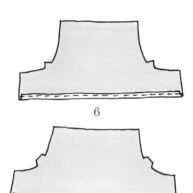

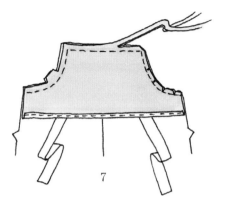

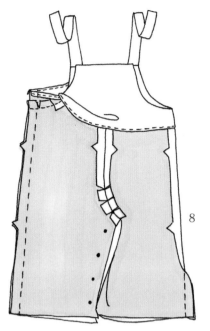

Facings

6   Turn under and press ¼in (6mm) along the lower
edge of the front and back facings. Stitch the
pressed edge down.

7   With right sides together, matching notches, pin
the back facing to the back. Stitch around the armhole
and top edge, taking care not to catch the straps in
the stitches. Trim the seam, snip the curves and cut
diagonally into the corners, taking care not to cut
into the stitching. Stitch the front facing to the front
in the same way.

Side seams

8   Press the facings to the inside. Open the facings out at
the armhole edges. With right sides together, matching
the notches, stitch the side seams right up to the top
edge of the facings. Press the seams open.

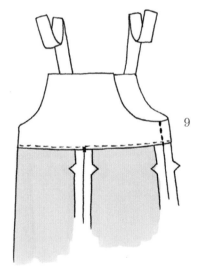

9   Press the facings back to the inside. On the right side of
the dungarees, run a line of stitches by hand or machine
along the seam, from the top to the lower edge of the
facing, to catch it down. Sew the facings down to the
seams at the centre front and centre back with a few
stitches by hand.

Hem

10 Turn under 1in (2.5cm) at the hem and press. Turn the
raw edge under and press, then stitch the hem.

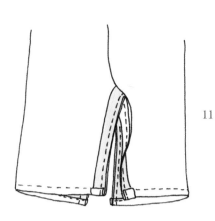

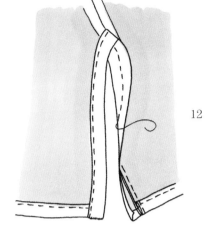

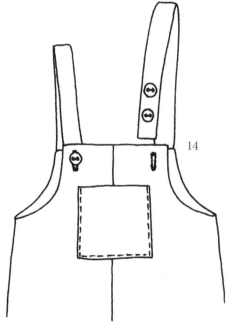

Inside-leg fastening

11 Make two 1⅛in (3cm)-wide bias binding strips *(see page 160)* to fit the length of each inner-leg edge at the front and back, allowing an extra ¾in (2cm) on the length of each strip. Trim the ends of the binding to a straight line. With right sides together, pin a bias strip to the inner-leg edge of the front and the back, turning under ⅜in (1cm) of the binding at each end. Stitch in place, allowing a ¼in (6mm) seam.

12 Press the seam towards the binding and press the bias strip to the inside. Turn under the raw edge and stitch. Slipstitch the ends of the binding to the edge of the hem.

Finishing off

13 Sew snap fasteners to the front and back inside legs *(see page 165)* at the medium dots.

14 Work buttonholes by hand or machine *(see page 163)* in the front. Sew two buttons securely *(see page 165)* to each strap, indicated on the pattern by an 'X'.

pants

These gorgeous little bloomers cover a nappy.
They can be made plain, or you can adapt them
with frills or an appliquéd bear.

The following guide shows how much material you will need for an average-sized child.			
FABRIC WIDTH (WITHOUT NAP)	**6–12 MONTHS**	**1–2 YEARS**	**2–3 YEARS**
36in (90cm)	⅔yd (0.6m)	¾yd (0.7m)	¾yd (0.7m)
45in (115cm)	⅔yd (0.6m)	¾yd (0.7m)	¾yd (0.7m)
60in (150cm)	⅔yd (0.6m)	¾yd (0.7m)	¾yd (0.7m)
Frills (in both main and contrast fabric)	5½ x 32½in (14 x 82.5cm)	5½ x 33in (14 x 84cm)	5½ x 33½in (14 x 85cm)

Suggested fabrics
Cotton shirting, batiste,
lightweight linen, chambray

Sewing notions
- Thread to match fabric
- 3 lengths of ¼in (6mm)-wide
  elastic to fit around the waist and
  each leg comfortably with an extra
  ¾in (2cm) on each one
- Bodkin or safety pin

For the appliquéd bear
- Fusible web interfacing
- 5 x 5in (13 x 13cm) fabric
  for bear face
- 1½ x 1½in (4 x 4cm) contrast
  or matching fabric for muzzle
- Stranded embroidery thread
  in brown
- Embroidery needle

Seam allowances
Take ⅝in (1.5cm) seam allowances
throughout, unless otherwise stated.

Finished measurements
Length from waist at side seam:
6–12 months: 7¼in (18.5cm)
1–2 years: 7¾in (20cm)
2–3 years: 8¼in (21cm)

Pattern piece on sheet B
36 Pants (cut 1 in main fabric)
The bear template can be found
on page 168.

**36in (90cm), 45in (115cm) and
60in (150cm) wide**

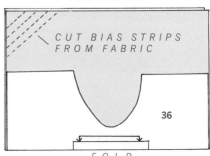

SELVEDGES

CUT BIAS STRIPS
FROM FABRIC

36

FOLD

Key

Key

☐ Right side of fabric

☐ Wrong side of fabric

1

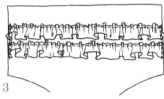

2

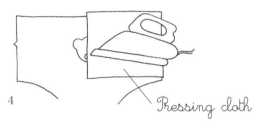

3

4 ✗ Pressing cloth

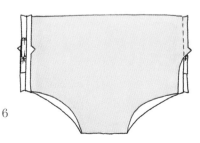

5

6

Instructions

Frills (optional)

1 Cut the strips of main and contrast fabric in half lengthways, so they each measure 2¾in (7cm) wide. With right sides of one main and one contrast strip together, stitch along the two long edges, allowing a ⅜in (1cm) seam. Join the remaining strips in the same way.

2 Turn right side out and press. Run two rows of gathering stitches *(see page 156)*, by hand or using a long machine stitch, working one row ⅜in (1cm) from the top edge and the other ¼in (6mm) above it. Pull up the gathering stitches to fit the back of the pants along the lines indicated on the pattern.

3 Adjust the gathers and pin the frills in place along the lines on the back of the pants, either with the main fabric side or contrast fabric side facing out. Tack the edges of the frills to the sides of the pants. Stitch ¼in (6mm) from the top of the frill. Remove the gathering stitches.

Appliquéd bear (optional)

4 Trace the template of the bear head and muzzle separately onto the paper side of the fusible web interfacing. Following the manufacturer's instructions, apply the fusible web interfacing to the back of the chosen fabrics *(see page 145)*. Cut out the shapes and position the appliqué on the back of the right side of the pants, as indicated on the pattern. Use a damp pressing cloth under the iron when fusing the shapes to the garment.

5 Use a narrow zigzag machine stitch or hand-embroidered buttonhole stitch to finish the edges *(see pages 151 and 167)*. Using three strands of embroidery thread, embroider the features with satin stitch for the eyes and nose and straight stitch for the mouth *(see page 167)*.

Side seams

6 With right sides together, stitch the front and back together at the side seams, sewing through the edges of the frills if applicable. Press seams open. Remove the tacking stitches.

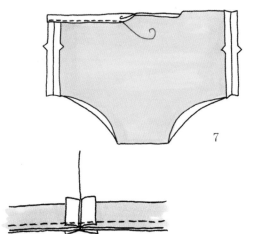

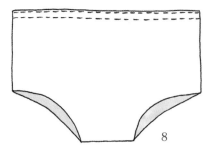

7

8

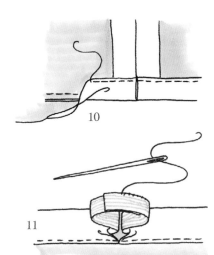

9

10

11

Waist

7 Turn under and press ¾in (2cm) at the waist. Turn under the raw edge and stitch, leaving a small opening near the side seam to insert the elastic.

8 Topstitch *(see page 151)* close to the top edge of the waist. This will help prevent the elastic from twisting inside the casing.

Legs

9 Cut 1in (2.5cm)-wide bias strips from the fabric to make bias binding *(see page 160)* to fit around the legs, allowing extra for ⅜in (1cm) turnings on each to neaten. Starting at the side seam of the pants, with right sides together, pin the bias binding to the leg and stitch in place allowing a ¼in (6mm) seam and turning under ⅜in (1cm) at each end of the binding.

10 Press the seam towards the binding and press the bias strip to the inside. Turn under the raw edge and stitch.

11 Using a bodkin or a safety pin, insert the elastic through the openings around the waist and legs. Adjust to fit. Overlap ⅜in (1cm) at the ends of the elastic so it lays flat. Stitch the ends together securely by hand or machine.

12 Push the ends of the elastic into the waistband and leg binding. Stitch the opening in the waistband by machine. Handsew the turned ends of the leg binding to close.

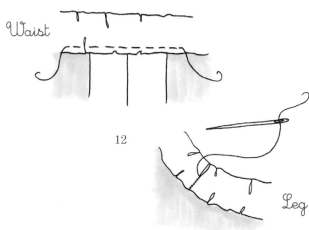

Waist

12

Leg

trousers & shorts

These trousers or shorts feature front pockets and a mock fly. The waistband is flat at the front and elasticated at the back, and so can be adjusted to fit as the wearer grows.

The following guide shows how much material you will need for an average-sized child.

FABRIC WIDTH (WITHOUT NAP)	1 YEAR OLD	2 YEAR OLD	3 YEAR OLD
36in (90cm)	Trousers: 1⅛yd (1m) Shorts: ¾yd (0.7m)	Trousers: 1¼yd (1.1m) Shorts: ⅞yd (0.8m)	Trousers: 1¼yd (1.1m) Shorts: ⅞yd (0.8m)
45in (115cm)	Trousers: ⅞yd (0.8m) Shorts: ⅔yd (0.6m)	Trousers: ⅞yd (0.8m) Shorts: ⅔yd (0.6m)	Trousers: 1yd (0.9m) Shorts: ¾yd (0.7m)
60in (150cm)	Trousers: ⅔yd (0.6m) Shorts: ½yd (0.45m)	Trousers: ⅔yd (0.6m) Shorts: ½yd (0.45m)	Trousers: ¾yd (0.7m) Shorts: ⅔yd (0.6m)
36in (90cm)-wide lightweight iron-on interfacing	¼yd (0.2m)	¼yd (0.2m)	¼yd (0.2m)

Suggested fabrics
Light- to medium-weight fabrics, corduroy, denim, canvas, linen

Sewing notions
- Thread to match fabric
- ½yd (0.45m) button elastic
- 2 x ⅝in (1.5cm) buttons
- 1 x ¾in (2cm) button
- Bodkin or safety pin

Finished measurements
Side length of trousers:
1 year: 19in (48.5cm)
2 years: 20½in (52cm)
3 years: 22in (55.5cm)
Side length of shorts:
1 year: 10¼in (26cm)
2 years: 12in (30cm)
3 years: 13¼in (33.5cm)

Pattern pieces on sheets E and F
37 Back (cut 2 in main fabric)
38 Front (cut 2 in main fabric)
39 Pocket (cut 2 in main fabric)
40 Pocket facing (cut 2 in main fabric)
41 Front waistband (cut 2 in main fabric, cut 2 in interfacing)
42 Back waistband (cut 1 in main fabric)

Open fabric out to cut back waistband

36in (90cm) wide – TROUSERS
SELVEDGES

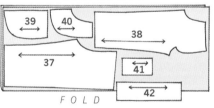

45in (115cm) wide – TROUSERS
SELVEDGES

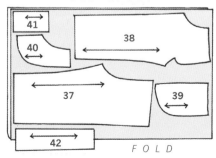

60in (150cm) wide – TROUSERS
SELVEDGES

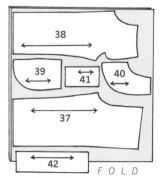

36in (90cm) wide – SHORTS

SELVEDGES

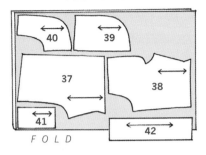

40   39

37

38

41

42

FOLD

45in (115cm) wide – SHORTS

SELVEDGES

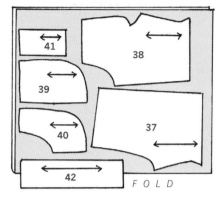

41

38

39

40

37

42

FOLD

60in (150cm) wide – SHORTS

SELVEDGES

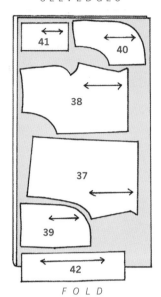

41   40

38

37

39

42

FOLD

Seam allowances

Take ⅝in (1.5cm) seam allowances throughout, unless otherwise stated.

Open fabric out to cut back waistband

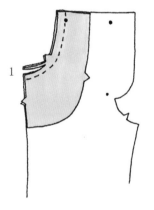
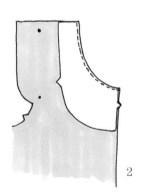

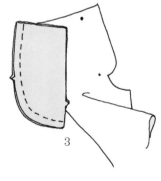
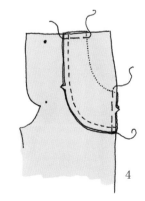

Instructions

Pockets

1   With right sides together, stitch the curved edge of the pocket facing to the trouser/shorts fronts. Trim the seams and snip the curves *(see page 153)*.

2   Turn the pocket facing to the inside and press. Topstitch *(see page 151)* close to the edge.

3   Lay the pocket facing away from the trouser/shorts front. With right sides together, stitch the curved edges of the pocket to the pocket facing.

4   Turn the pockets to the inside and press. Align the top and side edges of the pocket with the trouser/shorts front, matching the notches, and tack in place.

Key

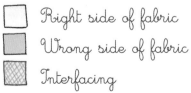

Right side of fabric

Wrong side of fabric

Interfacing

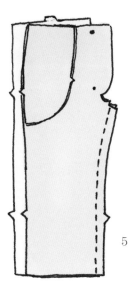

5

6

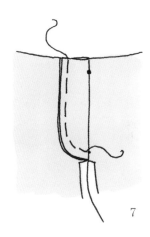

7

Join front to back

5   With right sides together, matching the notches, stitch the trouser/shorts front to the back along the inside leg seam. Press seam open.

6   With right sides together, matching notches and inside leg seam lines, stitch the crotch seam and fly placket of the left and right legs together, pivoting the needle at the small dot. Stitch a second row over the first to reinforce the seam. Trim the seam and snip the curves. Snip to the small dot at the front, taking care not to cut into the stitching. Press the crotch seam open from the front dot to the back waist.

Mock fly

7   Matching the dots at the centre front, press the fly placket to one side. Tack the fly placket in place over the stitched seam.

8   On the right side, topstitch through all layers, following the line of the tacking. Remove tacking stitches.

8

Side seams

9   With right sides together, matching the notches, stitch the side seams. Press the seams open. Remove tacking stitches from pockets at side seams.

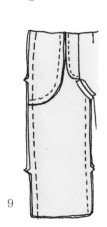

9

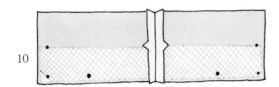

10

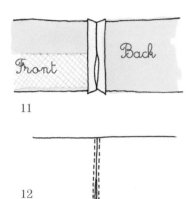

Front   Back

11

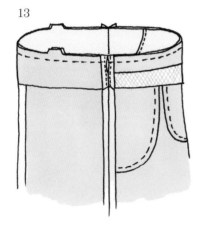

12

13

Waistband

10 Following the manufacturer's instructions, apply iron-on interfacing *(see page 145)* to the wrong side of the front waistband pieces, up to the fold line. With right sides together, matching notches, pin and stitch the waistband pieces together at the centre front. Press the seam open.

11 With right sides together, pin and stitch the front and back waistband together, leaving an opening between the small dots.

12 Press the seams open. Topstitch each side of the waistband side seams.

13 With right side of waistband to the wrong side of the trouser/shorts front, matching notches, dots and side seams, the large dot to the centre back seam and the centre front seam to the folded edge of the mock fly opening, pin and stitch through all layers, easing the front to fit the waistband. Press the waistband up. Trim the seam and press towards the waistband.

14 Press the waistband along the fold line. Press under a ⅝in (1.5cm) seam allowance. On the outside of the garment, pin the pressed edges of the waistband over the seams. Topstitch close to the pressed edges.

15 Topstitch close to the top edge of the waistband.

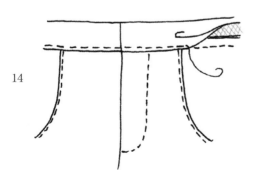

14

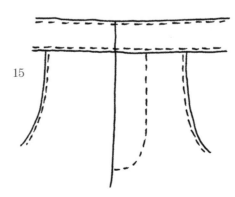

15

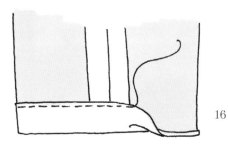

16

Hem

16 Turn under 1in (2.5cm) at the hem and press. Turn the raw edge under and press, then stitch the hem.

Finishing off

17 Sew a button securely *(see page 165)* to each side of the inside of the front waistband, ⅜in (1cm) from the side seam.

18 Use a bodkin or safety pin to thread the buttonhole elastic through the opening at the back waistband, fastening it to the buttons on each side. Trim the ends of the button elastic, allowing an extra ¼in (6mm) each side to turn under to neaten. To secure the ends of the elastic, turn under each end and slipstitch *(see page 151)* to the inside of the waistband. Adjust to fit.

19 Finish by sewing a decorative button to the waistband.

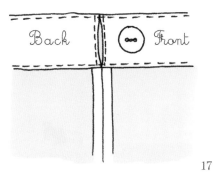

17

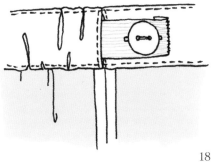

18

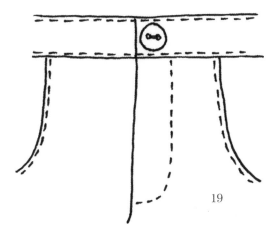

19

waistcoat

The waistcoat can be made as a reversible garment by using a similar weight for the main fabric and lining, and adding buttons to both sides to fasten.

The following guide shows how much material you will need for an average-sized child.

FABRIC WIDTH (WITHOUT NAP)	1 YEAR OLD	2 YEAR OLD	3 YEAR OLD
36in (90cm)	Main fabric: ¹/₂yd (0.45m) Lining fabric: ¹/₂yd (0.45m)	Main fabric: ¹/₂yd (0.45m) Lining fabric: ¹/₂yd (0.45m)	Main fabric: ¹/₂yd (0.45m) Lining fabric: ¹/₂yd (0.45m)
45in (115cm)	Main fabric: ¹/₂yd (0.45m) Lining fabric: ¹/₂yd (0.45m)	Main fabric: ¹/₂yd (0.45m) Lining fabric: ¹/₂yd (0.45m)	Main fabric: ¹/₂yd (0.45m) Lining fabric: ¹/₂yd (0.45m)
60in (150cm)	Main fabric: ¹/₂yd (0.45m) Lining fabric: ¹/₂yd (0.45m)	Main fabric: ¹/₂yd (0.45m) Lining fabric: ¹/₂yd (0.45m)	Main fabric: ¹/₂yd (0.45m) Lining fabric: ¹/₂yd (0.45m)
36in (90cm)-wide lightweight iron-on interfacing	¹/₃yd (0.3m)	¹/₃yd (0.3m)	¹/₃yd (0.3m)

Suggested fabrics
Linen, chambray, gabardine, poplin, corduroy, needlecord, denim
Lining: Cotton shirting, cotton-mix fabrics, lining fabrics

Sewing notions
- Thread to match fabric
- 3 x ⁵/₈in (1.5cm) buttons

Seam allowances
Take ⁵/₈in (1.5cm) seam allowances throughout, unless otherwise stated.

Finished measurements
Back length:
1 year: 10in (25.5cm)
2 years: 10½in (27cm)
3 years: 11in (28cm)

Pattern pieces on sheet D
43 Front (cut 2 in main fabric, cut 2 in lining fabric and 2 in interfacing following the line indicated on the pattern)
44 Back (cut 1 in main fabric, cut 1 in lining fabric)

Key

☐ *Right side of fabric*
▨ *Wrong side of fabric*
▥ *Interfacing*

36in (90cm), 45in (115cm) and 60in (150cm) wide

SELVEDGES

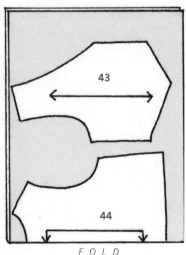

FOLD

Instructions

1   Following the manufacturer's instructions, apply iron-on interfacing *(see page 145)* to the wrong side of the left and right front pieces following the line on the pattern.

2   With right sides together, matching notches, stitch the front and back main fabric pieces at the shoulders. Repeat for the lining pieces. Press seams open.

Attach lining

3   With right sides together, matching notches and seams, pin and stitch the lining to the garment around the fronts, neck, armholes and lower edges, leaving the sides open. Trim the seams and snip the curves *(see page 153)*.

4   Turn right side out through a side opening in the back of the waistcoat and push the fronts out through the shoulders. Press well.

Side seams

5   With right sides together, matching notches, stitch the back and front main pieces at the side seams, leaving the lining open. Press seams open.

6   Reach in through one open side seam and pull the other side seam through. Stitch the side seam of the lining and push back in place.

7   Turn under the seam allowance on the remaining side seam of the lining and slipstitch *(see page 151)* to close.

Finishing off

8   Work buttonholes by hand or machine *(see page 163)* on the right front for a girl and left front for a boy, as indicated on the pattern. Overlap the front of the waistcoat, matching the centre front. Mark the position of buttons to correspond with the buttonholes. Attach the buttons to the left front for girl and right front for boy *(see page 165)*.

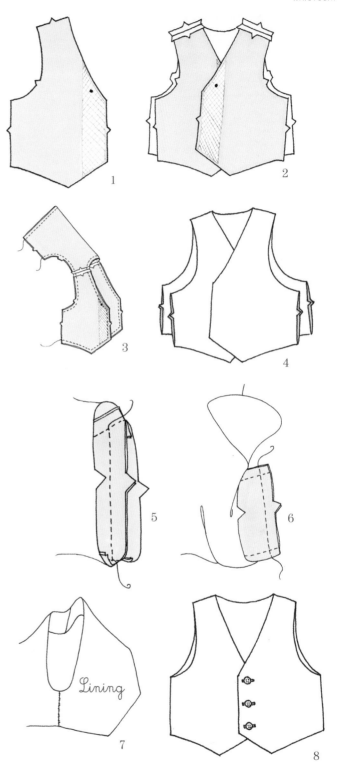

party dress

Any little girl will feel like a princess in this dress. Straps tie at the shoulders, the zip fastening is easy to do and the sash can be left unattached.

The following guide shows how much material you will need for an average-sized child.

FABRIC WIDTH (WITHOUT NAP)	1 YEAR OLD	2 YEAR OLD	3 YEAR OLD
36in (90cm)	Main fabric: 1¼yd (1.1m) Facing: ⅜yd (0.35m) Overskirt: ⅔yd (0.6m) Sash: ⅞yd (0.8m)	Main fabric: 1¼yd (1.1m) Facing: ⅜yd (0.35m) Overskirt: ¾yd (0.7m) Sash: ⅞yd (0.8m)	Main fabric: 1⅓yd (1.2m) Facing: ½yd (0.45m) Overskirt: ¾yd (0.7m) Sash: ⅞yd (0.8m)
45in (115cm)	Main fabric: 1¼yd (1.1m) Facing: ⅜yd (0.35m) Overskirt: ⅔yd (0.6m) Sash: ⅞yd (0.8m)	Main fabric: 1¼yd (1.1m) Facing: ⅜yd (0.35m) Overskirt: ¾yd (0.7m) Sash: ⅞yd (0.8m)	Main fabric: 1⅓yd (1.2m) Facing: ½yd (0.45m) Overskirt: ¾yd (0.7m) Sash: ⅞yd (0.8m)
60in (150cm)	Main fabric: 1yd (0.9m) Facing: ⅜yd (0.35m) Overskirt: ⅔yd (0.6m) Sash: ⅞yd (0.8m)	Main fabric: 1⅛yd (1m) Facing: ⅜yd (0.35m) Overskirt: ¾yd (0.7m) Sash: ⅞yd (0.8m)	Main fabric: 1¼yd (1.1m) Facing: ½yd (0.45m) Overskirt: ¾yd (0.7m) Sash: ⅞yd (0.8m)

Suggested fabrics
Main fabric: lightweight linen, satin, batiste, chambray
Facing: linen, cotton, cotton-mix fabric
Overskirt: tulle, net, lace
Sash: satin, silk

Sewing notions
- Thread to match fabric
- 8in (20.5cm) zip
- Hook and eye

Seam allowances
Take ⅝in (1.5cm) seam allowances throughout, unless otherwise stated.

Finished measurements
Length of underskirt:
1 year: 10¼in (26cm)
2 years: 10½in (27cm)
3 years: 11in (28cm)

Key

☐ *Right side of fabric*

▦ *Wrong side of fabric*

Pattern pieces on sheets C and D
45 Side bodice (cut 2 in main fabric, cut 2 in facing fabric)
46 Back bodice (cut 1 in main fabric, cut 1 in facing fabric)
47 Front bodice (cut 1 in main fabric, cut 1 in facing fabric)
48 Shoulder tie strap (cut 4 in main fabric)
49 Sash (cut 2 in sash fabric)
50 Skirt (cut 2 in main fabric, cut 2 in overskirt fabric)

60in (150cm) wide – MAIN FABRIC

SELVEDGES

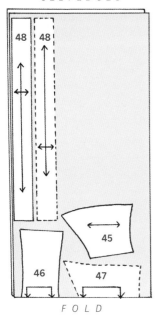

36in (90cm) and 45in (115cm) wide – MAIN FABRIC

SELVEDGES

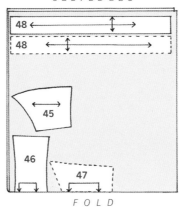

FOLD

Broken lines indicate reverse side of pattern

36in (90cm), 45in (115cm) and 60in (150cm) wide – FACING

SELVEDGES

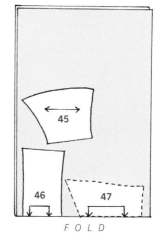

FOLD

36in (90cm), 45in (115cm) and 60in (150cm) wide – MAIN FABRIC and OVERSKIRT FABRIC

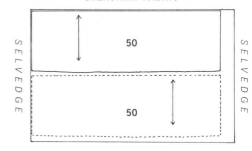

Open out fabric to cut skirt

36in (90cm), 45in (115cm) and 60in (150cm) wide – SASH

SELVEDGE

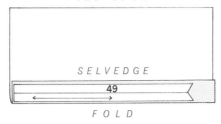

SELVEDGE

FOLD

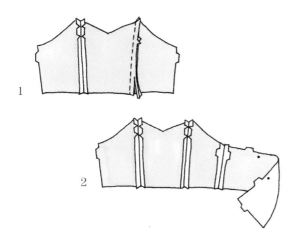

Instructions

Bodice

1 With right sides together, matching notches, stitch side fronts to front bodice. Repeat with the side-front facing and front-bodice facing pieces. Trim seams and notch curves *(see page 153)*. Press seams open.

2 With right sides together, matching notches, stitch the front to the back at the right-side seam, leaving the left side open for the zip fastening. Press seam open. Repeat for the facing.

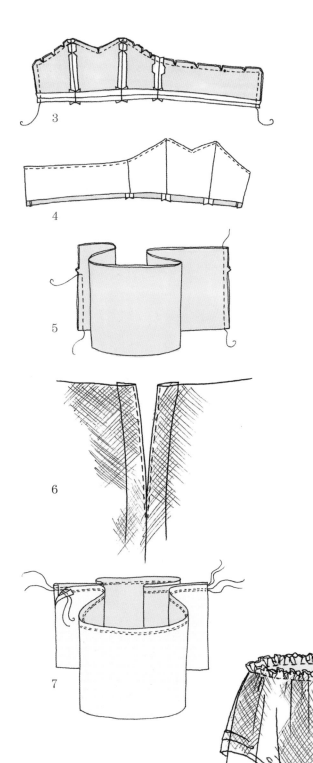

Attach facing

3   Press under ⅝in (1.5cm) on the lower edge of the bodice. With right sides of bodice and bodice facing together, matching notches and seams, pin and stitch the top and side edges together, leaving the lower edge open. Trim seams, snip curves, snip into the centre front and cut diagonally into the corners, taking care not to cut into the stitching.

4   Turn right side out and press. Topstitch *(see page 151)* close to the top edge of the bodice.

Skirt

5   With right sides together, stitch side seams of skirt in main fabric, leaving an opening above the notch on one side. This will be the underskirt. Trim seams and press open. Join the side seams in the same way on the overskirt. When pressing delicate fabric such as tulle, place a cloth between the iron and the fabric and press carefully using the lowest heat setting. It is advisable to test the iron on a scrap of the fabric first.

6   Turn under and press the seam allowance at the opening on both layers of skirt. Stitch ⅛in (3mm) from the edge of the opening on the overskirt only.

7   Run two rows of gathering stitches *(see page 156)* along the upper edge of the front and back of the underskirt, by hand or using a long machine stitch, working one row along the seam line and the other ¼in (6mm) inside the seam line. Repeat for the overskirt.

8   Pull up the gathering stitches on each layer of skirt separately to fit the lower edge of the bodice. Place the wrong side of the tulle skirt over the right side of the underskirt, matching the side seams and the edges of the opening. Adjust the gathers to fit, and tack in place at the top edge of the skirts.

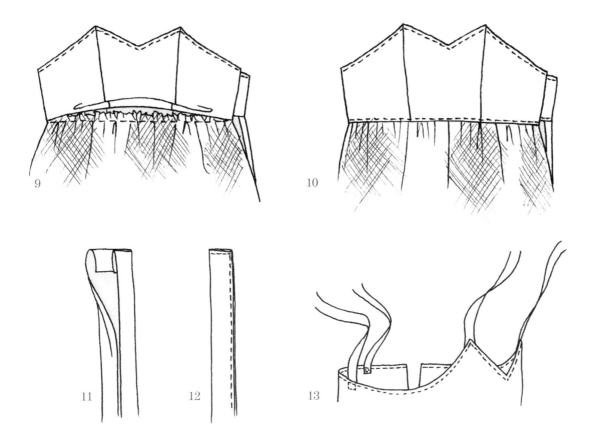

Attach skirt to bodice

9   With right side of bodice facing to wrong side of the gathered edge of the underskirt, matching the opening and side seams, pin and stitch together, sewing through all layers. With the iron set at the lowest heat, place a cloth over the overskirt and carefully press the seam towards the bodice.

10   On the outside of the garment, pin the pressed edges of the bodice over the seam. Topstitch close to the pressed edge.

Shoulder straps

11   On each strap, turn under ¼in (6mm) at both short edges, turn the long edges in to meet in the centre and press.

12   Fold the strip in half lengthways and topstitch near the edge.

13   Pin one end of each strap to the inside back of the bodice at the dots and the inside front at the seams, placing the end of the strap ⅜in (1cm) from the top edge of the bodice. On the right side of the garment, stitch the strap in place over the topstitching at the front and forming a small square of stitches, around ¼in (6mm) deep, at the back. Tie the front and back straps together in a bow at each shoulder, adjusting to fit.

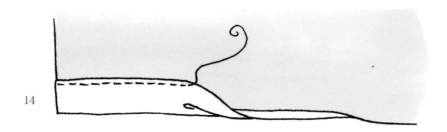

14

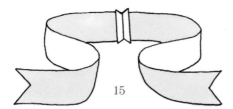

15

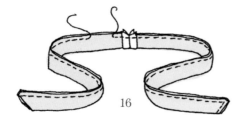

16

17

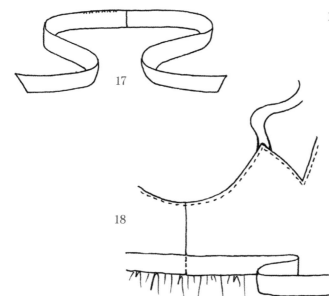

18

Hem

14 Turn under and press ⅝in (1.5cm) on the hem of the underskirt only. Turn under the raw edge, press and stitch. Leave the overskirt unhemmed.

Sash

15 With right sides together, stitch the short, straight edges of the two sash pieces to make one long length. Press the seam open.

16 With right sides together, fold the sash along the line indicated on the pattern. Stitch all around, leaving an opening on one long edge to turn. Trim the seams and cut diagonally across the corners, taking care not to cut the stitching.

17 Turn the sash right side out and press. Slipstitch *(see page 151)* the opening closed.

18 To attach the sash to the dress, place the sash against the bodice with the long seam at the lower edge lined up with the seam line of the waist. Align the short seam in the centre of the sash with the seam of the dress at the right side of the bodice. Run a line of stitches by hand or machine through the seam of the sash and the side seam of the bodice.

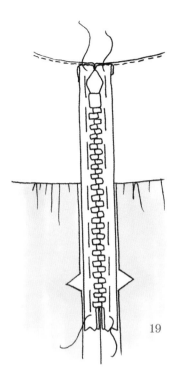

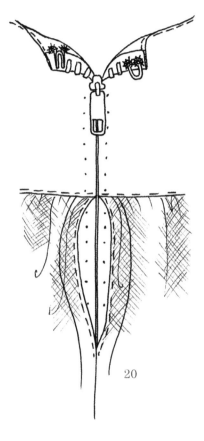

Insert zip

19 Turn the garment inside-out and, keeping the edges of the side opening together, place the closed zip face-down on the inside of the dress opening. Pin in position, placing the top of the zip at the top of the bodice and aligning the zip's teeth with the closed edges of the bodice and underskirt. Make sure both sides are even and the waist seam matches. Turn under the top edges of the zip tape and slipstitch in place. Tack the zip in place, leaving the overskirt opening free.

20 Turn the garment to the right side and, with thread doubled and coated with beeswax *(see page 141)*, stitch by hand with prick stitch *(see page 150)*, following the line of the tacking stitches, to attach the zip to the bodice and underskirt. Remove the tacking stitches. Sew a hook-and-eye fastening to the top of the bodice opening *(see page 165)*.

cape

For a contemporary take on Little Red Riding Hood's cape, this version is made in a deep red, felted wool mix with a contrasting French navy, polka-dot cotton lining.

The following guide shows how much material you will need for an average-sized child.

FABRIC WIDTH (WITHOUT NAP)	1 YEAR OLD	2 YEAR OLD	3 YEAR OLD
36in (90cm)	Main fabric: 1³/₈yd (1.3m) Lining fabric: 1yd (0.9m)	Main fabric: 1¹/₂yd (1.4m) Lining fabric: 1yd (0.9m)	Main fabric: 1¹/₂yd (1.4m) Lining fabric: 1¹/₈yd (1m)
45in (115cm)	Main fabric: 1¹/₈yd (1m) Lining fabric: ³/₄yd (0.7m)	Main fabric: 1¹/₄yd (1.1m) Lining fabric: ³/₄yd (0.7m)	Main fabric: 1¹/₄yd (1.1m) Lining fabric: ⁷/₈yd (0.8m)
60in (150cm)	Main fabric: 1yd (0.9m) Lining fabric: ²/₃yd (0.6m)	Main fabric: 1¹/₈yd (1m) Lining fabric: ²/₃yd (0.6m)	Main fabric: 1¹/₈yd(1m) Lining fabric: ²/₃yd (0.6m)
36in (90cm) iron-on woven interfacing	¹/₂yd (0.45m)	²/₃yd (0.6m)	²/₃yd (0.6m)

Suggested fabrics

Wool, tweed, needlecord, corduroy, velvet
For lining: cotton, cotton mix
Not suitable for diagonal prints

Sewing notions

- Thread to match fabric
- 3 x ⁷/₈in (2.25cm) buttons
- 1 x ³/₈in (1cm) snap fastening

Pattern pieces on sheet B

51 Front (cut 4 in main fabric, cut 2 in interfacing)
52 Back (cut 1 in main fabric, cut 1 in lining fabric)
53 Side front (cut 2 in main fabric, cut 2 in lining fabric)
54 Top collar (cut 1 in main fabric)
55 Under collar (cut 2 in lining fabric, cut 2 in interfacing)

Seam allowances

Take ⁵/₈in (1.5cm) seam allowances throughout, unless otherwise stated.

Finished measurements

Back length:
1 year: 15³/₄in (40cm)
2 years: 16³/₄in (42.5cm)
3 years: 17³/₄in (45cm)

36in (90cm) wide – MAIN FABRIC

SELVEDGES

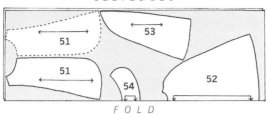

FOLD

45in (115cm) wide – MAIN FABRIC

SELVEDGES

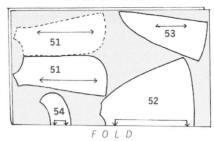

FOLD

60in (150cm) wide – MAIN FABRIC

SELVEDGES

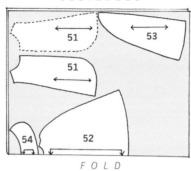

FOLD

36in (90cm) wide – LINING FABRIC

SELVEDGES

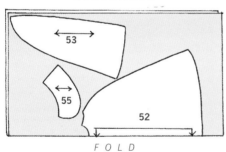

FOLD

60in (150cm) – LINING FABRIC

SELVEDGES

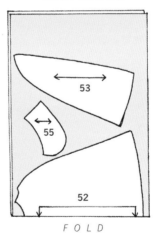

FOLD

45in (115cm) wide – LINING FABRIC

SELVEDGES

FOLD

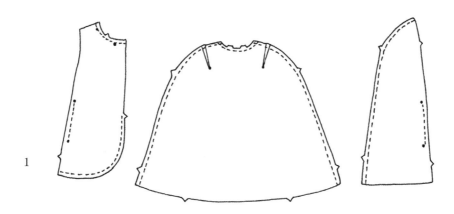

1

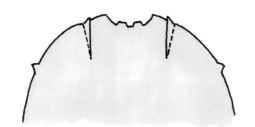

2

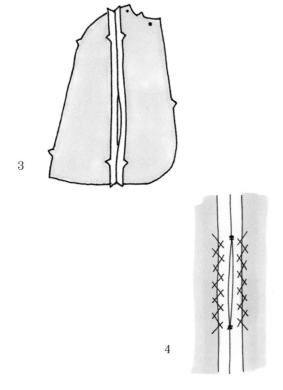

3

4

Instructions

1 Staystitch *(see page 151)* the neck edges of the front and back pieces and the front facings to prevent the fabric from stretching. Staystitch the side edges of the back and side fronts and the curved, lower edge of the fronts from the notch. Staystitch between the medium dots for the arm openings on the fronts, front facings, side fronts and side front linings.

2 Stitch the shoulder darts on the back *(see page 155)*. Press the darts towards the centre back.

3 With right sides together, matching notches, pin and stitch the side fronts to the front pieces, leaving an opening in the seam between the medium dots. The remaining front pieces will be used as facings.

4 Press the seam open and catch stitch *(see page 150)* the seam allowance down by hand at the open edges. On the inside, work a few stitches over each other by hand, to secure each end of the opening

Bound buttonholes

Work bound buttonholes next, on the right front of the cape *(see page 164)*. Hand-worked or machine buttonholes are added at the end, after making up the cape.

Key

☐ Right side of fabric

▨ Wrong side of fabric

▨ Interfacing

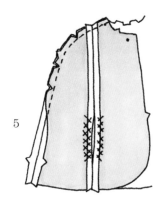

Collar

5 With right sides together, matching the dots, notches and lining up the dart to the front seam, stitch the back and fronts together. Trim the seams and notch the curves. Press the seams open.

6 Following the manufacturer's instructions, apply iron-on interfacing *(see page 145)* to the wrong side of the under-collar pieces. With right sides together, matching notches, pin and stitch the under-collar pieces together at the centre back. Press the seam open.

7 To ease in the fullness of the top collar, use a long machine stitch to work a line of stitching along the seam line of the outside edge.

8 With right sides together, matching notches and the medium dots at the centre front, pin the top collar to the under collar. Ease the top collar to fit by pulling the machine stitching. Stitch around the outer edges, leaving the neck edge open. Trim the seams and notch the curves *(see page 153)*.

9 Turn right side out and press, rolling the seam towards the under collar and aligning the raw edges. Tack the raw edges of the collar together.

10 With right side of the under collar to the right side of the cape, pin and tack the collar to the neck edge matching the notches and the small dots to the shoulder seams.

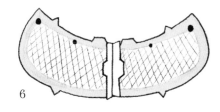

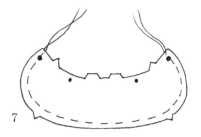

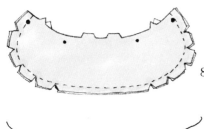

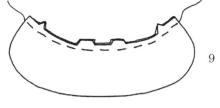

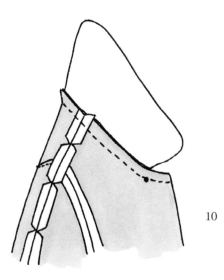

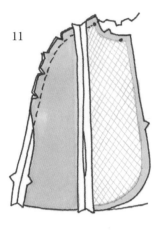

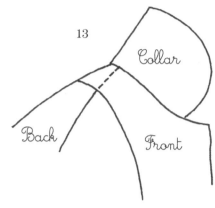

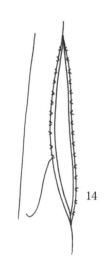

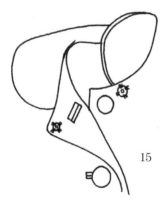

Linings and facings

11 Stitch and press the darts in the back of the lining as for the cape. Following the manufacturer's instructions, apply iron-on interfacing to the wrong side of the left and right front facings. With right sides together, matching notches, pin and stitch the side front linings to the front facings, leaving an opening in the seam between the medium dots. Press the seams open. Join lining side pieces to lining back and trim the seams, notch the curves and press as for cape.

12 With right sides of cape and lining together, matching the seams and pattern markings, pin and stitch all around the outer edges. Trim the seams, notch the curves and cut diagonally across the corners, taking care not to cut into the stitching.

13 Reach in through one of the openings at the side front, between the cape and lining, turn the work right side out and press. On the right side of garment, run a line of stitches by hand or machine along the shoulder seam, from the neck edge to where the front seam and dart meet, to catch the lining down.

14 On the inside, slipstitch the lining and facings to the edges of the cape at the opening. Finish by working buttonholes by hand or machine *(see page 163)* on the right front, as indicated on the pattern. If bound buttonholes were made, hem the facings around the buttonholes *(see page 164)*.

15 Lap the right front over the left, matching the centre front. Mark the position of buttons to correspond with the buttonholes. Attach the buttons to the left front. Sew the snap fastening to the cape front at the neck edge to hold the corner in place under the collar *(see page 165)*.

fairy wings

These wings hold their shape with a padding of wadding and heavy-weight interfacing. The quilted layers add delicate-looking detail.

The following guide shows how much material you will need for an average-sized child.

FABRIC WIDTH (WITHOUT NAP)	ONE SIZE TO FIT 1–3YRS
36in (90cm)	⁷⁄₈yd (0.8m)
45in (115cm)	³⁄₄yd (0.7m)
60in (150cm)	¹⁄₂yd (0.45m)
36in (90cm)-wide heavy-weight sew-in interfacing	¹⁄₂yd (0.45m)

Suggested fabrics
Cotton, linen, calico, silk, satin

Sewing notions
- Thread to match fabric
- 32½in (82.5cm) length of ⅜in (1cm) elastic
- 13 x 20in (33 x 51cm) wadding
- Tracing paper
- Dressmaker's carbon paper
- Pencil
- Bodkin or safety pin

Seam allowances
Take ⅜in (1cm) seam allowances throughout, unless otherwise stated.

Finished size
Wingspan:
Approximately 15¾in (40cm) at the widest part

Pattern pieces on sheet B
56 Fairy wings (cut 4 in main fabric, cut 4 in interfacing, cut 2 in wadding)

Instructions

1 Staystitch *(see page 151)* the shaped edges of each wing to prevent the fabric from stretching.

 Key

Right side of fabric

Wrong side of fabric

Interfacing

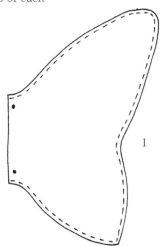

1

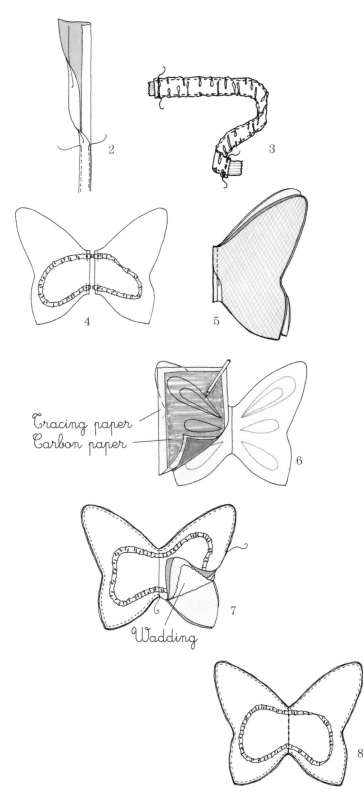

Tracing paper
Carbon paper

Wadding

Shoulder straps

2 Cut two 2 x 24in (5 x 61cm) strips from the fabric. Turn under and press ¼in (6mm) along each long edge. Fold in half lengthwise and press. Topstitch along *(see page 151)* each side, close to the edges.

3 Cut the elastic in two equal halves and use a bodkin or safety pin to thread the elastic through the straps. Adjust to fit, trim the excess elastic and stitch to secure at each end of the straps.

4 Tack each end of a shoulder strap to the right side of a wing at the dots indicated on the pattern. Tack the other strap in place on a second wing to make a pair. These will be the facings, and the remaining pair will be referred to as the wings.

Join pieces

5 Place the interfacing on the wrong side of the wings and the facings. With right sides together, stitch the pieces together at the centre seam, sewing through all layers. Press the seams open.

6 Transfer the quilting template to the wings by tracing the design onto tracing paper. Slip carbon paper, carbon side down, between the pattern and the right side of the right fairy wing. Trace over the design with a pencil. Flip the tracing paper and transfer the design onto the left fairy wing as for the right.

7 Sandwich the wadding between the interfaced side of the wings and facings, aligning the shaped edges. Pin and stitch the wings and facings together around the outside edges, allowing a ⅜in (1cm) seam and sewing through all layers.

8 Sew a line of stitches, by hand or machine, down the centre seam of the wings, taking care not to catch the shoulder straps in the stitches.

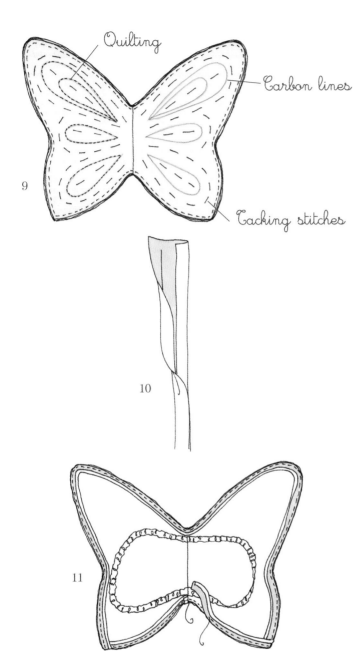

Quilting

9   Hold the layers of fabric and wadding in place with tacking stitches. Starting from the centre and working out towards the edges, work the quilted design by hand or machine on each wing, following the lines on the fabric. Take care the fabric doesn't pucker as you stitch. Remove the tacking stitches.

Binding

10   Cut 1½in (4cm)-wide bias strips from a 12 x 12in (30 x 30cm) piece of the fabric and sew the short edges together to make the binding *(see page 160)*. Press a ⅜in (1cm) seam allowance along each long edge. Fold the binding in half lengthways and press.

11   Turn under ⅜in (1cm) at the short end of the binding and align the fold with the centre seam at the lower edge of the wing facings. Open out one side of the binding and, with the right side of the binding to the facing, pin and stitch the creased edge of the binding to a ⅜in (1cm) seam allowance at the edges, overlapping the end and folding out the fullness of the binding at the corners *(see page 161)*.

12   Turn the binding to the right side of the wings to encase the seam allowances. Pin the pressed edge over the seams. Topstitch close to the pressed edges. Press the bound edges, but take care not to press the main part of the wings as the wadding will melt under a hot iron.

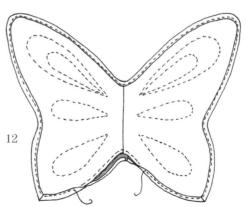

crown

This little crown is embellished with stencilled gems. Use the same colour fabric paint for all, or apply different shades for each gem.

The following guide shows how much material you will need for an average-sized child.

FABRIC WIDTH (WITHOUT NAP)	ONE SIZE TO FIT 1–3YRS
36in (90cm)	8in (20.5cm)
45in (115cm)	8in (20.5cm)
60in (150cm)	4½in (11.5cm)
36in (90cm)-wide heavy-weight iron-on interfacing	4½in (11.5cm)

Suggested fabrics
Medium- to heavy-weight cotton, linen, canvas

Pattern pieces on sheet C
57 Band (cut 1 in main fabric)
58 Point (cut 10 in main fabric, cut 5 in interfacing)

Seam allowances
Take ⅜in (1cm) seam allowances throughout, unless otherwise stated.

Sewing notions
- Thread to match fabric
- 1in (2.5cm) elastic to fit the circumference of the head, with an extra ¾in (2cm)

For the stencilled gems
- Freezer paper
- Pencil
- Craft knife
- Cutting mat
- Fabric paint
- Sponge or paintbrush

Finished size
To fit 1–3 years, up to 19¾in (50cm) head circumference

Key
- ☐ Right side of fabric
- ▨ Wrong side of fabric
- ▦ Interfacing

36in (90cm), 45in (115cm) wide

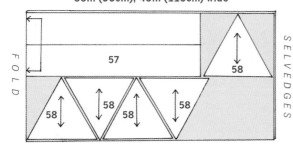

60in (150cm) wide

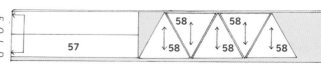

Instructions

Stencilled gems

1 Cut five 2 x 2in (5 x 5cm) pieces of freezer paper and use a pencil to trace the gem design on each piece. Prepare the stencils *(see page 166)*, cutting one for each gem. Follow the instructions on page 166 to stencil the gems on the band of the crown, positioning them as marked on the pattern. When the stencils are dry, place a dry cloth over the top and fix the ink by ironing well for a few minutes on both sides at the highest heat suitable for the fabric.

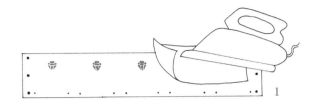

Interfacing

2 Following the manufacturer's instructions, apply iron-on interfacing *(see page 145)* to the wrong side of five of the triangular pieces. These will be the facings.

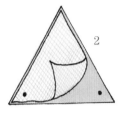
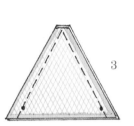

Crown points

3 With right sides together, stitch each of the triangular facings to the remaining triangular pieces, allowing ⅜in (1cm) seams and leaving the lower edges open to turn. Trim the seams and cut the tip of the triangle to a straight line, taking care not to cut into the stitching. This will reduce the bulk and enable the piece to lay flat.

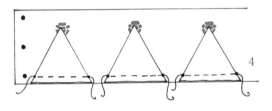

4 Turn the pieces right side out and press. Pin the right side of the point facings to the right side of the lower edge of the band, matching the small dots and aligning the raw edges. Tack in place.

Band

5 Press under ⅜in (1cm) on one short edge. With right sides together, fold the band along the line indicated on the pattern and stitch the long edges together, allowing a ⅜in (1cm) seam.

Finishing off

6 Turn right side out and press well. Use a bodkin or safety pin to thread the elastic through the opening in the band. Overlap ¾in (2cm) at the ends of the elastic so it lays flat. Stitch the ends together securely by hand or machine.

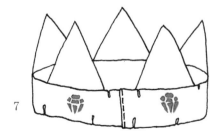

7 Push the elastic inside the band. Slip the raw edge of the band under the pressed edge, matching the medium dots. Topstitch *(see page 151)* the opening, close to the pressed edge.

pirate hat

The hat has a wide-shaped brim trimmed with white binding and an appliquéd skull and crossbones. You could also stencil the design using fabric paint.

The following guide shows how much material you will need for an average-sized child.

FABRIC WIDTH (WITHOUT NAP)	ONE SIZE TO FIT 1–3YRS
36in (90cm)	1yd (0.9m)
45in (115cm)	1yd (0.9m)
60in (150cm)	½yd (0.45m)
36in (90cm)-wide heavy-weight sew-in interfacing	½yd (0.45m)

For the binding
½ x ½yd (0.45 x 0.45m) of white fabric

Suggested fabrics
Light- to medium-weight cotton

Sewing notions
- Thread to match fabric

For the appliquéd skull and crossbones
- Fusible web interfacing
- 4½ x 6in (11.5 x 15cm) white cotton fabric
- White sewing thread

Seam allowances
Take ⅜in (1cm) seam allowances throughout, unless otherwise stated.

Finished sizes
To fit 1–3 years, up to 19¾in (50cm) head circumference

36in (90cm) and 45in (115cm) wide

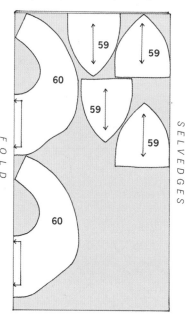

60in (150cm) wide – MAIN FABRIC

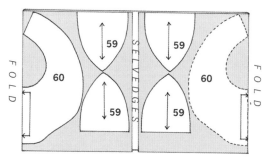

Broken lines indicate reverse side of pattern

Pattern pieces on sheet D
59 Crown (cut 8 in main fabric)
60 Brim (cut 2 in main fabric, cut 1 in interfacing)
The skull and crossbones template can be found on page 169

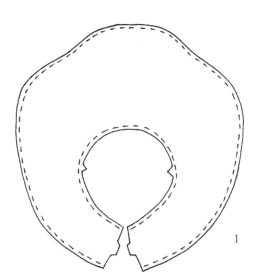

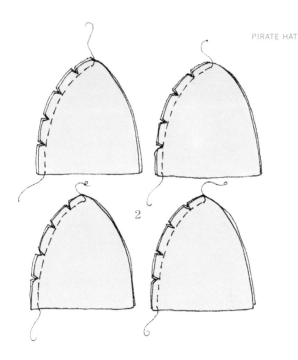

Instructions

1 Staystitch *(see page 151)* around the curved edges of the crown and brim pieces to prevent the fabric from stretching.

Crown

2 With right sides together, pin and stitch two of the crown pieces together at a time along one curved edge. Trim and notch the seams *(see page 153)*. Press the seams to one side. This will give you four half-crown pieces.

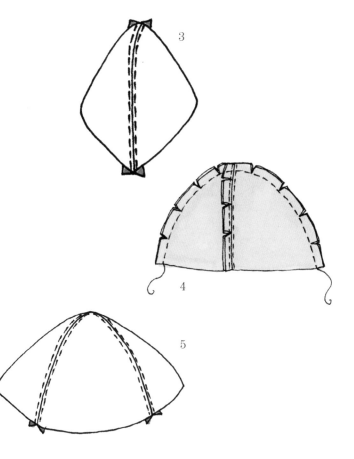

3 Topstitch *(see page 151)* along each side of the seams.

4 With right sides together, matching the seams, pin and stitch two halves of the crown pieces together from the lower edge, up to the top and down the other side. Trim and notch the seams. Press the seams to one side.

5 Topstitch along each side of the seam. This will give you two finished crowns. One will be the outer crown and the other will be the lining.

Key

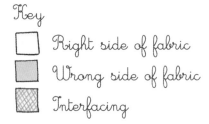

☐ Right side of fabric

▨ Wrong side of fabric

▨ Interfacing

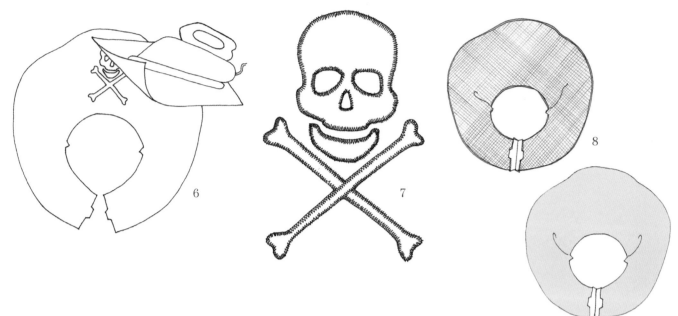

Appliquéd skull and crossbones

6   Trace the skull and crossbones template from page
    169 onto the paper side of the fusible web interfacing.
    Following the manufacturer's instructions, apply the
    fusible web interfacing to the back of the white fabric
    (see page 145). Cut out the shapes carefully, removing
    the eye and nose pieces. Position the pieces, as
    indicated on the pattern, on the right side of one of the
    brims. Use a damp pressing cloth under the iron when
    fusing the design to the garment.

7   Use a narrow zigzag machine stitch or hand-embroidered
    buttonhole stitch *(see pages 151 and 167)* to finish all
    the edges of the appliqué.

Brim

8   Align the interfacing to the wrong side of the brim that
    was not appliquéd. This will be the upper part of the
    brim and the appliquéd piece will be on the underside.
    With right sides together, pin and stitch the short edges
    of each of the brim pieces.

9   Press the seams open. Topstitch close to each side
    of the seam lines on both brim pieces.

10 With wrong sides together, matching the notches and
    seams, tack together the two brim pieces around the
    outer and inner edges.

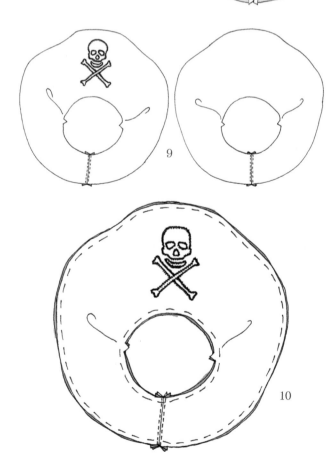

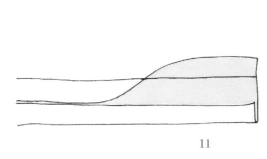

11

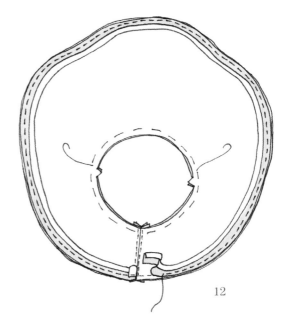

12

Binding

11 Cut 1½in (4cm)-wide bias strips from the white fabric
and sew the short edges together to make the binding
(see page 160). Press a ⅜in (1cm) seam allowance along
each long edge.

12 Turn under ⅜in (1cm) at the short end of the binding
and align the folded edge with the seam at the back of
the upper side of the brim. Open out one side of the
binding and, with the right side of the binding to the
underside of the brim, pin and stitch the creased
edge of the binding to the ⅜in (1cm) seam allowance,
overlapping the end. Press the seam towards the binding.

13 Press the binding to the underside of the brim to
encase the seam allowance. Pin the pressed edge
over the seams. Topstitch close to the pressed edges.
Press the bound edges.

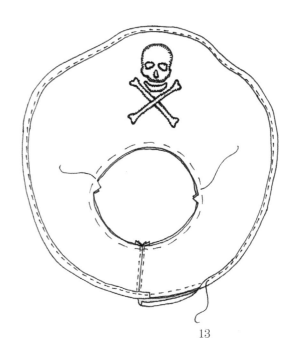

13

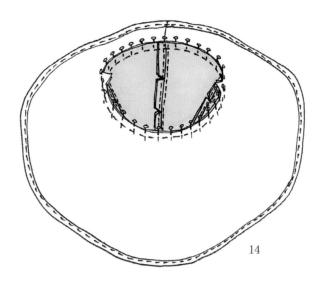

Lining

14 Pin the underside of the brim to the right side of the lower edges of the lining, matching the notches, the back seam and the centre front of the brim to the seams of the crown lining. Use plenty of pins to ease the fabric and stitch in place.

15 Press under ⅜in (1cm) on the lower edge of the crown. With wrong sides of the crown and lining together, matching the seams, pin the pressed edge of the crown over the seam joining the lining to the brim. Stitch in place close to the pressed edge.

16 Fold the front of the brim up against the crown and hold in place with a few stitches worked over each other by hand. Hide the stitches by sewing neatly through the upper brim only, working them from just above where the top of the skull would be, and right through the seam of the crown.

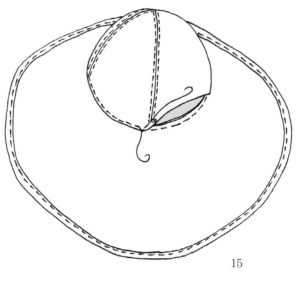

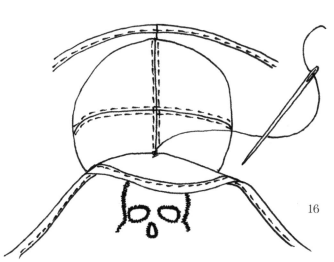

tabard

This attractive tabard can be adapted for any dressing-up character with the stencilled emblems bringing the imaginary world of play to life.

The following guide shows how much material you will need for an average-sized child.

FABRIC WIDTH (WITHOUT NAP)	1 YEAR OLD	2 YEAR OLD	3 YEAR OLD
36in (90cm)	Main fabric: ²/₃yd (0.6m)	Main fabric: ²/₃yd (0.6m)	Main fabric: ²/₃yd (0.6m)
45in (115cm)	Main fabric: ²/₃yd (0.6m)	Main fabric: ²/₃yd (0.6m)	Main fabric: ²/₃yd (0.6m)
60in (150cm)	Main fabric: ²/₃yd (0.6m)	Main fabric: ²/₃yd (0.6m)	Main fabric: ²/₃yd (0.6m)

For the binding
20 x 20in (51 x 51cm) of contrast fabric

Suggested fabrics
Calico, cotton, linen

Sewing notions
• Thread to match fabric
For the stencilled emblems
• Freezer paper
• Pencil
• Craft knife
• Cutting mat
• Fabric paint
• Sponge or paintbrush

Pattern pieces on sheet C
61 Front (cut 1 in main fabric)
62 Back (cut 1 in main fabric)
The eagle, skull and crossbones and castle templates can be found on page 169

36in (90cm), 45in (115cm) and 60in (150cm) wide

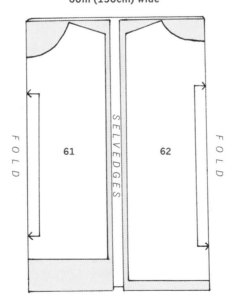

Seam allowances
Take ⅝in (1.5cm) seam allowances on shoulder seams and ⅜in (1cm) seam allowances on bound edges.

Finished measurements
Front length:
1 year: 17½in (44.5cm)
2 years: 18½in (47cm)
3 years: 19½in (49.5cm)
Back length:
1 year: 19½in (49.5cm)
2 years: 20½in (52cm)
3 years: 21½in (54.5cm)

1

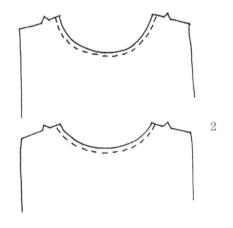

2

Instructions

Stencilled emblems

1   Cut 8 x 8in (20.5 x 20.5cm) square from the freezer paper. Trace the chosen design from the template onto the paper side of the freezer paper. Mark the dots on the freezer paper and prepare the stencil *(see page 166)*. Remember to keep the separate eye and nose pieces of the skull in a safe place until you are ready to use them. Position the stencil on the front of the tabard, matching the dots. Follow the instructions on page 166 to stencil the emblem. When the stencil is dry, place a dry cloth over the top and fix the ink by ironing well for a few minutes on both sides at the highest heat suitable for the fabric.

2   Staystitch *(see page 151)* the neck edges of the back and front at the ⅜in (1cm) seam allowance.

Join front to back pieces

3   With right sides together, stitch the front to the back at the shoulders. Press the seams open.

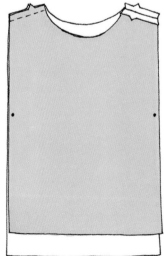

3

Binding

4 Cut 1½in (4cm)-wide bias strips from the contrast fabric and sew the short edges together to make the binding *(see page 160)*. Press a ⅜in (1cm) seam allowance along each long edge.

5 To bind the neck edge, turn under ⅜in (1cm) at the short end of the binding and align the folded edge with the shoulder seam. Open out one side of the binding and, with the right side of the binding to the inside of the garment, pin and stitch the creased edge of the binding to a ⅜in (1cm) seam allowance at the neck edge, overlapping the end. Press the seam towards the binding.

6 To bind the edges of the tabard, turn under ⅜in (1cm) at the short end of the binding. Starting at the shoulder seam, with the right side of the binding to the inside of the garment, pin and stitch the creased edge of the binding to a ⅜in (1cm) seam allowance at the edges of the tabard, overlapping the end and folding out the fullness of the binding at the corners *(see page 161)*. Press the seams towards the binding.

7 Turn the binding at the neck and edges of the tabard to the right side of the garment to encase the seam allowances. Pin the pressed edge over the seams. Topstitch *(see page 151)* close to the pressed edges. Press the bound edges.

Ties

8 Cut four 15¾in (40cm) lengths from the bias strip. Turn under and press the short ends and fold the strips in half lengthways so the pressed edges meet.

9 Topstitch along all four sides of the ties, close to the edges of each one.

10 On the inside of the garment, align one short end of the tie with the edge of the binding at the seam. Stitch the ties at the medium dots on each side of the front and back, forming a small square of stitches.

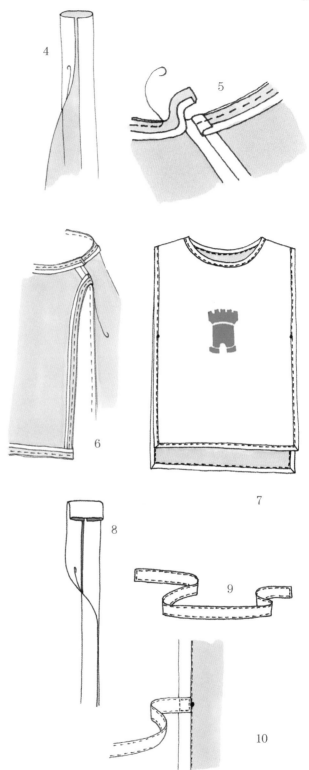

feather headdress

Experiment with colour and texture to create a variety of feathers for this headdress. The headband is elasticated and embellished with Suffolk puff patchwork pieces.

Fabric required
- 23⅝ x 3½in (60 x 9cm) for the headdress band
- 2 pieces of 7 x 3in (18 x 7.5cm) fabric for each of the seven feathers
- 3 x circles of fabric for decoration, 3in (7.5cm) diameter

Suggested fabrics
Cotton shirting, tweed, linen

Sewing notions
- Thread to match fabric
- Contrasting thread
- 14 pieces of 7 x 3in (18 x 7.5cm) heavy-weight iron-on interfacing
- 1in (2.5cm) elastic to fit the circumference of the head comfortably, with an extra ¾in (2cm)

Seam allowances
Take ⅜in (1cm) seam allowances throughout, unless otherwise stated.

Finished size
To fit 1–3 years, up to 19¾in (50cm) head circumference

Pattern pieces on sheet A
63 Small feather (trace 2 onto interfacing, see step 1)
64 Medium feather (trace 2 onto interfacing, see step 1)
65 Large feather (trace 3 onto interfacing, see step 1)
66 Band (cut 1 in main fabric)
67 Decoration (cut 3 in main or contrast fabric)

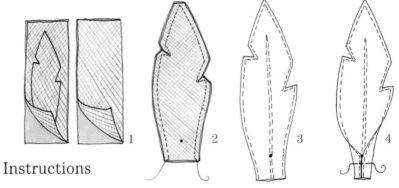

Instructions

Feathers

1 Trace three large feathers and two each of the medium and small feathers onto the matt side of seven pieces of iron-on interfacing. Following the manufacturer's instructions, apply the iron-on interfacing (see page 145) to the wrong side of one the fabric pieces chosen for each feather. Apply the blank interfacing to the wrong side of the remaining fabric pieces.

2 With right sides together, pin the two pieces of fabric together. Using a small machine stitch, sew along the lines drawn on the interfacing. Trim the seam to within ⅛in (3mm) of the stitching. Snip into the inverted corners and cut straight across the pointed ends, taking care not to cut into the stitching, so the shape lays flat when turned right side out (see page 153).

3 Turn the feather right side out, using a knitting needle to push out the corners, and press well. With contrasting thread, topstitch (see page 151) close to the edges and run two rows of stitches down the centre, as indicated on the pattern, for the quill of the feather.

4 Turn in the corners at each side of the feather to meet in the middle and stitch down by hand or machine, around ⅝in (1.5cm) from the lower edge. This will give them shape and prevent them flopping. Turn some of the feathers over before doing this to reverse the shape and create more variation.

Key
☐ Right side of fabric
▨ Wrong side of fabric
▨ Interfacing

Band

5   With the folded side of the feathers facing up and aligning the raw edges, arrange the feathers on the right side of the band, matching the dots. Place one of the three biggest feathers at the large, centre-front dot. Position the remaining two large feathers at the small dot on each side of the centre front, the medium feathers at the dots next to the large feathers and finally, the small feathers at the last dots. Tack the feathers in place on the band.

6   Press under ⅜in (1cm) at one short end of the band. Press the feathers up and press under a ⅜in (1cm) turning at the top and lower edges.

7   With wrong sides together, fold the band at the line indicated on the pattern, matching the pressed edges. Pin and topstitch close to the top edge, stitching through the folded ends of the feathers sandwiched in between.

8   Press the band and topstitch close to the lower edge.

Elastic

9   Use a bodkin or safety pin to thread the elastic through the opening in the band. Overlap ¾in (2cm) at the ends of the elastic so it lays flat. Stitch the ends together securely by hand or machine.

10 Push the elastic inside the band. Slip the raw edge of the band under the pressed edge, matching the medium dots. Topstitch the opening, close to the pressed edge.

Decoration

11 To make the Suffolk puff, turn under ¼in (6mm) on the edge of a circular piece of fabric, fasten the thread under the fold and, turning the edge of the fabric as you go, run a line of ¼–⅜in (6mm–1cm)-long stitches by hand close to the turned edge.

12 Draw up the thread to gather the circles and sew a few stitches over each other to secure the gathers. Stitch the decorations securely by hand to the front of the band at the triangles marked on the pattern, sewing between the folds of the gathers to hide the stitches.

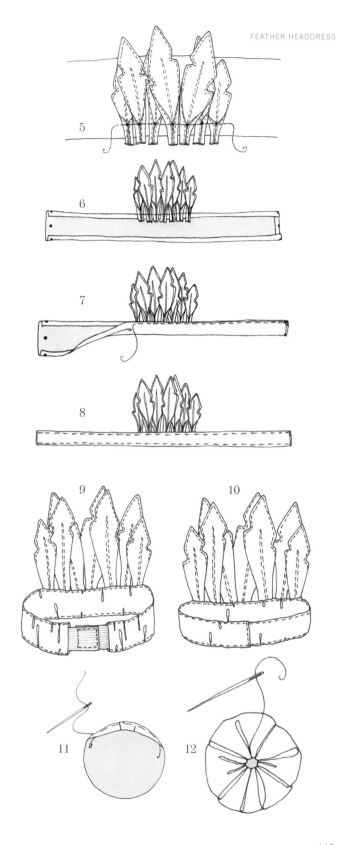

animal masks

These animal masks are a great addition to the dressing-up box – simple accessories that will transform boys and girls into their forest and feline friends.

The following guide shows how much material you will need for an average-sized child.

FABRIC WIDTH (WITHOUT NAP)	ONE SIZE TO FIT 1–3YRS
36in (90cm)	¼yd (0.2m)
45in (115cm)	¼yd (0.2m)
60in (150cm)	¼yd (0.2m)

Suggested fabrics
Medium-weight cotton, linen, calico

Sewing notions
- Thread to match fabric
- 13¾in (35cm) length of ⅜in (1cm) elastic
- Heavy-weight sew-in interfacing for rabbit: 6 x 12in (15 x 30cm); for fox and cat: 4 x 6in (10 x 15cm)
- Dressmaker's carbon paper
- Pencil

For the cat and rabbit
- Stranded embroidery thread
- Embroidery needle

For the fox
- 4 pieces of 2 x 4in (5 x 10cm) white fabric
- 4 pieces of 2 x 4in (5 x 10cm) heavy-weight iron-on interfacing

Seam allowances
Take ⅜in (1cm) seam allowances throughout, unless otherwise stated.

Finished size
To fit 1–3 years, up to 19¾in (50cm) head circumference

Pattern pieces on sheet E
68 Animal mask interlining (cut 2 in main fabric)
69 Fox mask (cut 2 in main fabric)
70 Cat and rabbit masks (cut 2 in main fabric)
71 Cat mask ear (cut 4 in main fabric, cut 2 in interfacing)
72 Rabbit mask ear (cut 4 in main fabric, cut 2 in interfacing)
73 Fox mask ear (cut 4 in main fabric, cut 2 in interfacing)

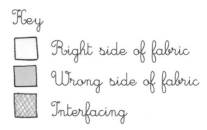

Key
☐ Right side of fabric
▨ Wrong side of fabric
▧ Interfacing

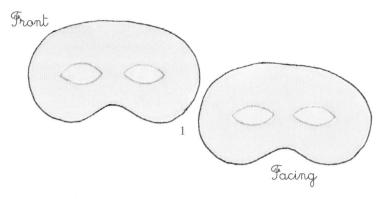

Instructions

1   Transfer the lines of the eyes from the pattern to the wrong side of the two main mask pieces by placing dressmaker's carbon paper between the pattern and the fabric and drawing over the lines with a pencil. One of these will be the front of the mask and the other will be the facing.

2   Staystitch *(see page 151)* around the curved outer edges of the front, facing and the two interlining pieces to prevent the fabric from stretching.

Whiskers (cat and rabbit only)

3   Transfer the lines of the whiskers onto the right side of the front of the mask by placing dressmaker's carbon paper between the pattern and the fabric and drawing over the lines with a pencil. Using two strands of embroidery thread, embroider the whiskers in chain stitch *(see page 167)*.

Interlining

4   With right sides together, align the outer edges of the front and the interlining pieces and pin together. The interlining pieces will overlap at the centre. Stitch around the eyes, following the carbon lines traced from the pattern. Carefully cut out the fabric inside the eyes and trim to ⅛in (3mm) from the stitching. Snip into the corners and around the edges of each eye, taking care not to cut into the stitching.

5   Turn right side out by threading each piece of interlining through the eye, and press.

6   With wrong sides together, stitch the interlinings together at the centre seam, taking care not to catch the front of the mask in the stitches. Press the seam open. Tack the outer edges of the mask and interlinings together.

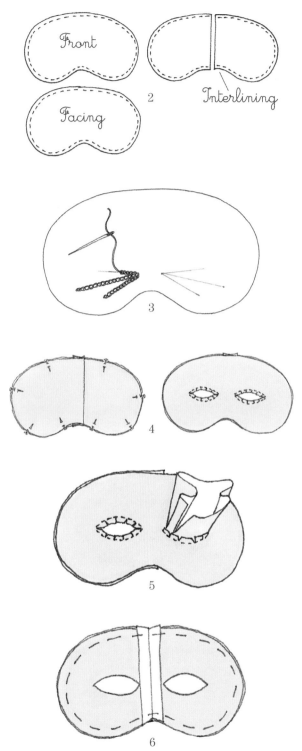

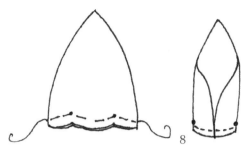
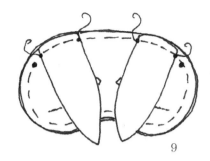

Ears

7   Place the ears right sides together, with the interfacing on the wrong side of each pair of ears. Stitch around the two sides, sewing through all layers and leaving the lower edge open. Trim the seams, notch the curves *(see page 153)* and cut across the point at the tip of the ear. Turn the ears right side out so the interfacing is on the inside and press.

Rabbit ears only

8   Tack the lower edges of the rabbit's ear together. Turn in the corners at each side of the ear to meet in the middle and stitch just inside the ⅜in (1cm) seam line. This will give the ears shape and also help to prevent them flopping.

All ears

9   Align the raw edges and tack the ears to the right side of the mask at the small dots indicated on the pattern. If making the rabbit mask, make sure the folded side of the ear is facing down.

Elastic casing

10 Cut a 2 x 19½in (5 x 49.5cm) strip from the fabric. Turn under and press ¼in (6mm) along each long edge. Fold in half lengthwise and press. Topstitch *(see page 151)* each side, close to the edges.

11 Use a bodkin or safety pin to thread the elastic through the casing. Adjust to fit, trim the excess elastic and stitch to secure at each end.

12 Tack each end of the casing to the right side of the mask at the medium dots indicated on the pattern.

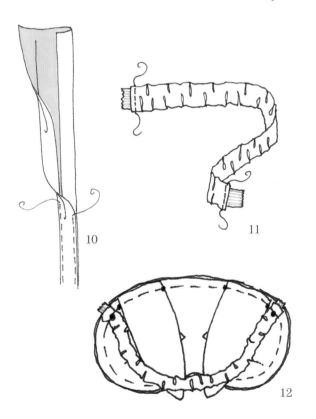

Facing

13 Stitch around the eyes on the wrong side of the facing, following the carbon lines. Cut a straight line from one corner of each eye to the other in the facing. Snip the fabric on each side of the slash up to the stitches. Press the snipped fabric to the wrong side along the line of stitches.

14 With right sides together, the elastic casing and ears sandwiched in between, pin and stitch the facing to the mask, all around the outer edges. The length of the casing and tips of the rabbit's ears can be pulled through the eyeholes to the outside of the mask to prevent them getting caught in the stitches. Trim the seam, notch the outward curves and snip the inward curves.

15 Carefully pull the mask right side out through one of the eyeholes in the facing and press well. Slipstitch *(see page 151)* the pressed edges of the facing down around the eyes.

Fox markings

16 Transfer each side of the design separately onto the matt side of two of the iron-on interfacing pieces, one piece for each side of the fox's white markings. Following the manufacturer's instructions, apply the iron-on interfacing *(see page 145)* to the wrong side of two of the fabric pieces. Apply the other two pieces of interfacing to the wrong side of the two remaining fabric pieces. Cut out both of the traced designs, following the carbon lines on the interfacing.

17 With the interfaced sides together, pin each of the cut-out designs to the remaining interfaced fabric pieces. Use a narrow zigzag machine stitch or hand-embroidered buttonhole stitch *(see pages 151 and 167)* to finish the edges. Cut around the edges close to the stitches, taking care not to cut into the stitching.

18 Pin the shapes in place on the front of the mask. Topstitch ⅛in (3mm) from the edge of the pieces, working all the way around. The stitches will go off the sides of the main part of the mask but will catch the fox's white markings down near the whiskery ends.

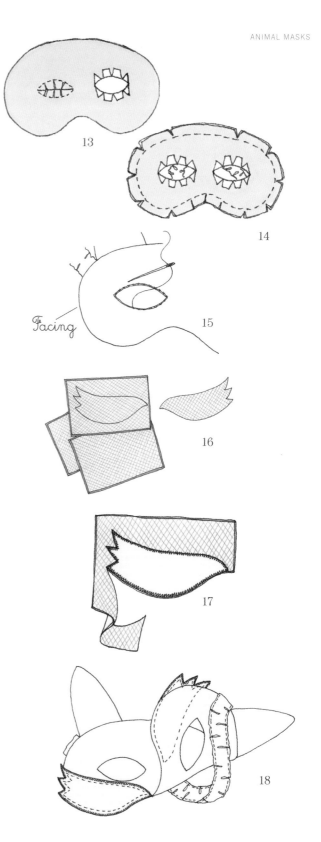

13

14

Facing   15

16

17

18

sun & rain hats

You can use different fabrics to make this hat suitable for rain or shine. Why not make both so your child will have a hat to wear whatever the weather?

The following guide shows how much material you will need for an average-sized child.

FABRIC WIDTH (WITHOUT NAP)	ONE SIZE TO FIT 1–3YRS	
	SUN HAT	RAIN HAT
36in (90cm)	Main fabric: ¹/₂yd (0.45m)	Main fabric: ²/₃yd (0.6m)
	Lining fabric: ³/₈yd (0.35m)	Lining fabric: ¹/₄yd (0.2m)
45in (115cm)	Main fabric: ³/₈yd (0.35m)	Main fabric: ²/₃yd (0.6m)
	Lining fabric: ¹/₃yd (0.3m)	Lining fabric: ¹/₄yd (0.2m)
60in (150cm)	Main fabric: ¹/₃yd (0.3m)	Main fabric: ²/₃yd (0.6m)
	Lining fabric: ¹/₃yd (0.3m)	Lining fabric: ¹/₄yd (0.2m)

Suggested fabrics

Sun hat: cotton, linen
Rain hat: PUL (polyurethane laminate) fabric
Lining: cotton, cotton blend

Sewing notions

- Thread to match main fabric and lining
- Snap fastening (optional)

Seam allowances

Take ³/₈in (1cm) seam allowances throughout, unless otherwise stated.

Finished size

To fit 1–3 years, up to 19¾in (50cm) head circumference

Pattern pieces on sheet C

74 Crown (cut 4 in main fabric, cut 4 in lining fabric)
75 Brim (for sun hat: cut 2 in main fabric and 2 in lining fabric, for rain hat: cut 4 in main fabric)

For the tie fastening (A) cut two 17½ x 1⅜in (44.5 x 3.5cm) strips in main fabric

45in (115cm) and 60in (150cm) wide – RAIN HAT MAIN FABRIC

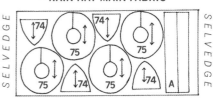

36in (90cm), 45in (115cm) and 60in (150cm) wide – RAIN HAT LINING

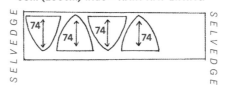

36in (90cm) wide – RAIN HAT MAIN FABRIC

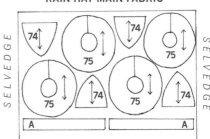

36in (90cm) wide – SUN HAT MAIN FABRIC

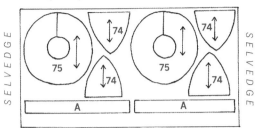

36in (90cm) wide – SUN HAT LINING

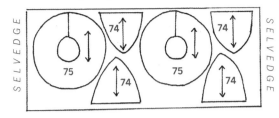

45in (115cm) wide – SUN HAT MAIN FABRIC

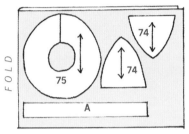

45in (115cm) and 60in (150cm) wide – SUN HAT LINING

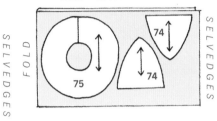

60in (150cm) wide – SUN HAT MAIN FABRIC

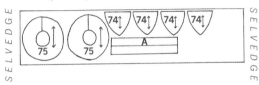

Key
Right side of fabric
Wrong side of fabric

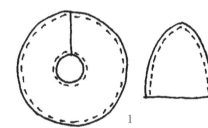

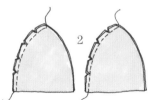

Instructions

1 Staystitch *(see page 151)* around the curved edges of the crown and brim pieces to prevent the fabric from stretching.

Crown

2 With right sides together, pin and stitch two of the main fabric crown pieces together at a time, along one curved edge. Trim and notch the seams *(see page 153)*. Press the seams to one side on the sun hat. If making a rain hat, do not use an iron on the coated side of the fabric.

3 Topstitch *(see page 151)* along each side of the seam.

4 With right sides together, matching the seams, pin and stitch the two halves of the main fabric crown pieces together from the lower edge, up to the top and down the other side. Trim and notch the seam. Press the seams to one side. Do not use an iron on the coated side of the PUL fabric, if you are using this.

5 Topstitch along each side of the seam.

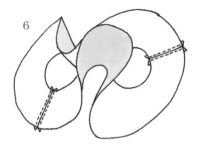

Brim

6 With right sides together, pin and stitch both the short edges of the two circular brim pieces to form one larger ring. Repeat for the remaining two brim pieces. This will give you an inner and outer brim piece. Press seams open, but if using PUL fabric, do not use an iron on the coated side. Topstitch close to each side of the seam lines on both inner and outer brim pieces.

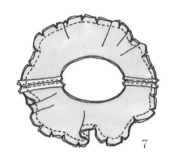

7 With right sides together, matching the notches and seams, pin and stitch the two brim pieces around the outer edge. Trim the seam and notch the curve. Turn the brim right side out and press. Do not use an iron on the coated side of the PUL fabric.

8 Topstitch around the outside of the brim, close to the edge. With wrong sides together, tack the inside edges of the brim to hold them together.

Tie fastening

9 Cut two 17½ x 1⅜in (44.5 x 3.5cm) strips in main fabric. On each strip of fabric, turn under ¼in (6mm) at one short edge; turn the long edges in to meet in the centre and press. Do not use an iron on the coated side of the PUL fabric.

10 Fold the strip of fabric in half lengthways and press. Topstitch near the edge.

11 Position both ties in line with the seams of the inner brim piece and tack in place, aligning the raw edge of the tie to the raw edge of the inside of the brim.

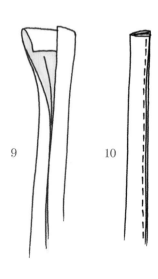

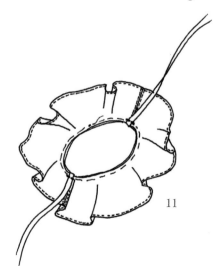

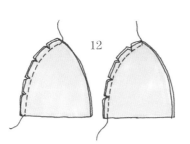

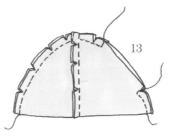

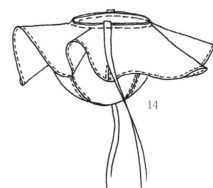

Lining

12 With right sides together, pin and stitch two of the crown lining pieces together at a time, along one curved edge. Trim and notch the seams. Press the seams to one side.

13 With right sides together, matching the seams, pin and stitch the two halves of the crown lining pieces together from the lower edge, up to the top and down the other side, leaving an opening of around 4¾in (12cm). Trim and notch the seam. Press the seams to one side.

14 Pin the outer brim against the right side of the crown with the inner brim, ties attached, facing up. Position the seams of the brim to the centre of the panels, as indicated by the dot on the pattern, on each side of the hat. The seams of the crown will form an 'X' over the top of the head. Use plenty of pins to ease the fabric of the brim in place. Sew together, taking care not to catch the extra fabric of the brim in the stitches.

15 With right sides of the crown and lining together and the brim sandwiched in between, pin the lining to the main fabric inside the seam joining the crown to the brim. Match the seams on the crown and lining and keep the brim and ties tucked neatly inside the two pieces. Stitch in place along the seam line, working over the previous row of stitches. Trim the seams and snip the curves.

16 Turn right side out and slipstitch *(see page 151)* together the opening inside the lining. Push the lining inside the crown of the hat.

17 The brim can be held in place up against the crown of the hat by working a few neat stitches by hand over the topstitching on the outer brim and through the crown. Alternatively, sew on a snap fastening *(see page 165)* to fasten the brim to the crown.

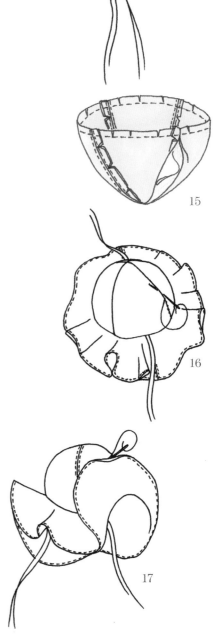

dolls

These projects are a great way to use up the small remnants from the larger projects in the book. You can dress the dolls up in tiny versions of the garments.

Suggested fabrics

Assorted remnants, such as cotton shirting, linen, calico and tulle

Sewing notions

- Thread to match fabric
- Toy stuffing
- Stranded embroidery thread in chosen colours for eyes, cheeks/ whiskers and doll's lips
- Embroidery needle

For dolls
- 6in (15cm) length of ⅛in (3mm)- wide elastic
- Bodkin or small safety pin

For wings (optional)
- Heavy-weight sew-in interfacing
- Tracing paper
- Dressmaker's carbon paper

Pattern pieces on sheet B

76 Doll head (cut 2 in main fabric)
77 Doll wing (cut 4 in main fabric, cut 2 in interfacing)
78 Doll trousers (cut 2 in main fabric)
79 Doll foot (cut 2 in main fabric)
80 Doll hand (cut 2 in main fabric)
81 Doll body (cut 2 in main fabric)
82 Doll leg (cut 2 in main fabric)
83 Boy doll sleeve (cut 2 in main fabric)
84 Rabbit and girl doll arm (cut 2 in main fabric)
85 Rabbit toy back body (cut 1 in main fabric)

86 Rabbit toy front body (cut 1 in main fabric)
87 Rabbit toy ear (cut 4 in main fabric)
88 Rabbit toy tail and doll corsage (cut 1 for each in main fabric)
89 Rabbit toy leg (cut 2 in main fabric)

To see how much fabric you need, refer to the appropriate column.

GIRL DOLL

Head and arms	7¾ x 15¾in (20 x 40cm)
Legs	6¾ x 9½in (17 x 24cm)
Body	5½ x 7¾in (14 x 20cm)
Skirt	6⅓ x 15in (16 x 38cm) each in fabric and tulle
Corsage	4 x 4in (10 x 10cm)

BOY DOLL

Head, legs and hands	9½ x 15in (24 x 38cm)
Sleeves and body	5½ x 13¾in (14 x 35cm)
Trousers	12 x 15¾in (30 x 40cm)
Bow tie	Bow: 2¾ x 4¾in (7 x 12cm)
	Knot: 2 x 2in (5 x 5cm)

GIRL OR BOY DOLL

Hair	13¾ x 13¾in (35 x 35cm)
Feet	5 x 6in (13 x 15cm)
Wings (optional)	5½ x 15¾in (14 x 40cm)

RABBIT

36in (90cm)-wide fabric (without nap)	⅓ yd (0.3m)

Seam allowances

Take ⅜in (1cm) seam allowances on the dolls and the rabbit toy.
Take ⅝in (1.5cm) seam allowances on the skirt and trousers.

Finished sizes

Approximately 18in (45.75cm) tall (not including doll's hair or rabbit's ears)

Instructions

Doll's head, body, hands and feet

1   With right sides together, stitch the seam joining the head to the body on both the identical front and back pieces. For the boy doll, stitch the seam joining the sleeve to the hand. Stitch the seam joining the leg to the foot. Press the seams towards the head, hands and feet.

Doll and rabbit's arms and legs

2   With right sides together, fold the arms and legs lengthways at the line indicated on the pattern, aligning the edges. Stitch the ⅜in (1cm) seams to the dots, leaving the top ends open. Trim the seam, notch the outward curves and snip into the inverted corners *(see page 153)*.

3   Turn the arms and legs right side out. Stuff the arms and legs firmly with toy stuffing, filling them to around ⅝in (1.5cm) from the raw edges and using a pencil to push the stuffing right into the ends of the hands and feet. Stitch straight across each of the top edges at the ⅜in (1cm) seam line.

Join legs to body

4   With the seams of the legs facing the sides of the body, matching the medium dots, pin the legs in place to the lower edge on the right side of the back of the body, aligning the raw edges. Stitch the legs to the body along the ⅜in (1cm) seam line.

Join doll's head

5   Turn under and press the ⅜in (1cm) seam allowances at the lower edge and down each side of the body. With right sides together, stitch around the shoulders, neck and head. Trim the seam, notch the outward curves and snip the inward curves. Turn right side out and press.

Key

Right side of fabric
Wrong side of fabric
Interfacing

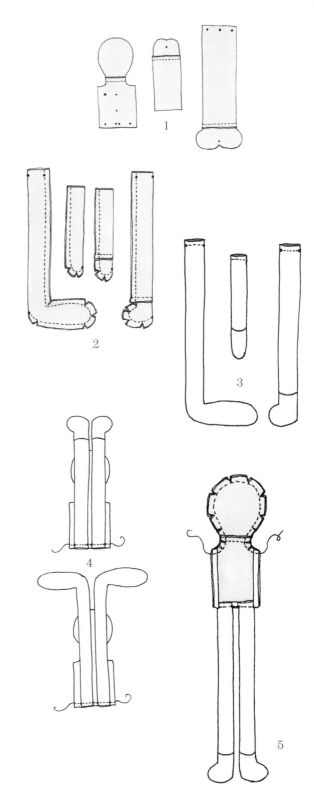

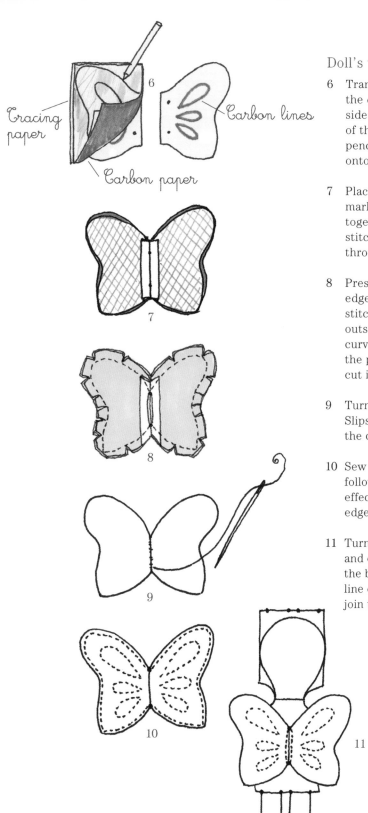

Tracing paper

Carbon lines

Carbon paper

Doll's wings (optional)

6   Transfer the pattern to one pair of the wings by tracing the design onto tracing paper. Slip carbon paper, carbon side down, between the pattern and the right side of the right fairy wing. Trace over the design with a pencil. Flip the tracing paper and transfer the design onto the left fairy wing as for the right.

7   Place the interfacing on the wrong side of the carbon-marked pair of wings. With right sides of wings together and sandwiched between the interfacing, stitch the pieces together at the centre seam, sewing through all layers. Press the seams open.

8   Press under ⅜in (1cm) seam allowance on the straight edge of each remaining wing. With right sides together, stitch the two pairs of wings together all around the outside edges. Trim the seam, notch the outward curves, snip the inward curves and cut straight across the points at the tips of the wings, taking care not to cut into the stitches.

9   Turn the wings right side out through the opening. Slipstitch *(see page 151)* together the opening at the centre seam.

10 Sew the design on the wings by hand or machine, following the lines on the fabric to produce a quilted effect. Topstitch *(see page 151)* close to the outside edges of the wings.

11 Turn the front of the body up so it lies under the head and out of the way. Pin the wings to the right side of the back of the body, matching the small dots. Run a line of stitching down each side of the centre seam to join the wings to the body.

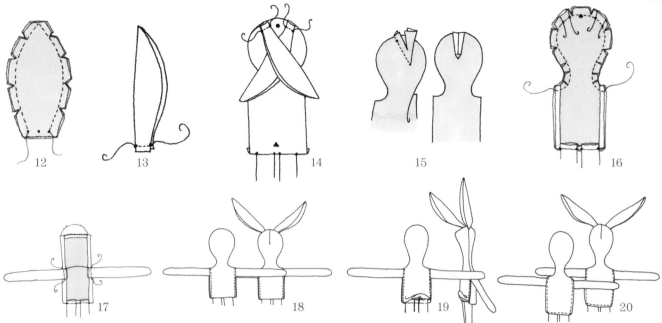

Rabbit's ears

12 With right sides together, stitch the two sides of the rabbit's ear, leaving the lower edge open. Trim the seams, notch the curves and cut across the tip of the ear, taking care not to cut into the stitching.

13 Turn the ears right side out and press. Fold the ears in half lengthways and tack across the lower edges.

14 With the folds of the ears facing towards the large dot, tack the ears in place to the right side of the back of the rabbit's head at the small dots.

Rabbit's head

15 Stitch the dart at the front of the head. Trim seam to ⅜in (1cm) and press open *(see page 155)*.

16 Turn under and press the ⅜in (1cm) seam allowances at the lower edge and down each side of the body. With right sides together, matching the seam with the large dot at the top of the head, stitch around the shoulders, neck and head, sewing through the ears at the same time. Keep the ears tucked in and away from the seams so that only the lower edges of the ears are stitched. Trim the seam, notch the outward curves and snip the inward curves. Turn right side out and press.

Join arms to doll and rabbit's body

17 With the seams of the arms facing down, tack the arms in place to the wrong side of the back of the body, aligning the raw edges and positioning the top of the arm right up against the shoulder seam.

18 With right sides together, pin the pressed edges together at the sides of the body, enclosing the top ends of the arms. Topstitch each side, close to the pressed edges. Move the wings to one side, if applicable. Remove the tacking stitches.

19 Stuff the head and body firmly, using a pencil to push the stuffing through the neck opening. Insert plenty of stuffing into the neck to prevent it flopping. Fill the doll to around ⅜in (1cm) from the pressed lower edge.

20 With right sides together, pin the pressed edges together at the lower edge of the body, enclosing the top ends of the legs. Tack in place and topstitch close to the pressed edges. This is a bit fiddly due to the stuffing in the body and legs so can be stitched by hand, if preferred. Remove the tacking stitches.

Rabbit tail and doll's corsage

21 Make a Suffolk puff for the rabbit's tail or corsage by following Step 11 of the feather headdress on page 113. Draw up the thread to gather the circle of fabric and sew a few stitches over each other to secure the gathers. Sew the piece securely by hand at the triangle marked on the pattern, stitching between the folds of the gathers to hide the stitches.

Embroidered features

22 Using two strands of embroidery thread, sew the eyes and the doll's mouth with satin stitch *(see page 167)*. Work a cross stitch *(see page 167)* for the rabbit's mouth with the centre at the point of the dart. Embroider cross stitches for the cheeks or whiskers, working a small 'x' over a large '+' shape.

Doll's hair

23 Cut 1in (2.5cm)-wide bias strips from the 13¾ x 13¾in (35 x 35cm) square of fabric chosen for the hair. Fabric that is cut on the bias tends to fray less, so is ideal for the doll's hair. Trim the ends to straighten the edges and then cut the strips to around 4 x 5½in (10 x 14cm) lengths. Form a length of fabric into a loop and secure with a few stitches.

24 Working around the seam of the head first, attach each loop to the head, sewing into the point where the strip of fabric crosses over and leaving the loop free to form a curl. Work a few stitches over each other, through the loops and into the head to secure the curls. After covering the seam, continue sewing the curls over the back of the head until the doll has a full head of curly locks.

Skirt

25 With right sides together, stitch the short edges together on both the main fabric layer of the skirt and the tulle layer, allowing a ⅝in (1.5cm) seam. Trim the seams. Press the seam of the main fabric layer open. Place a cloth between the iron and the tulle and press carefully on the lowest heat setting.

26 Turn under and press ⅝in (1.5cm) on the hem of the main fabric layer only. Turn under the raw edge, press and stitch.

27 Place the wrong side of the tulle skirt over the right side of the underskirt, matching the seams. Pin and stitch along the ⅝in (1.5cm) seam allowance at the top edge to join the two layers.

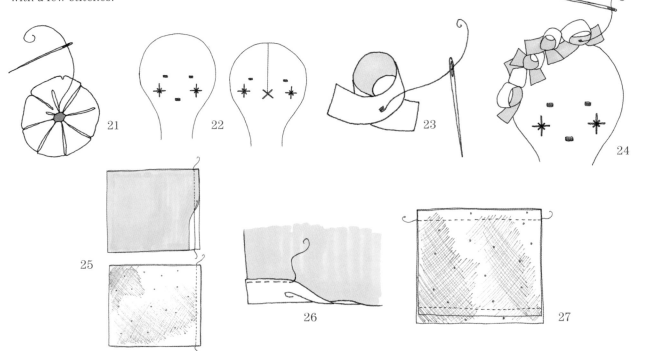

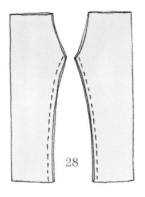

28

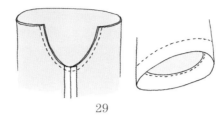

29

30

Trousers

28 With right sides together, stitch together the inside-leg seams.

29 With right sides together, slip one trouser leg inside the other and align the centre front and back, matching the seams. Stitch from the top edge at the waist, through the inside leg seam and right up to the waist edge on the opposite side. Turn right side out and press. Turn under and press ⅝in (1.5cm) on the hems of the legs. Turn under the raw edge, tack and stitch by hand or machine. Remove the tacking stitches.

Skirt and trousers

30 Turn under and press the ⅝in (1.5cm) seam allowance at the waist. Turn under the raw edge and press. (If working with tulle, press the fabric carefully under a cloth on the lowest heat setting as before.) Pin and stitch close to the pressed raw edge to form a narrow casing for the elastic, leaving a ¾in (2cm) opening at the back seam.

31 Use a bodkin or a small safety pin to insert the elastic through the opening in the waist casing at the back of the skirt or trousers. Adjust to fit, knot or stitch the ends of the elastic together and push it back into the waist casing. Stitch the opening in the waist to close.

Bow tie

32 With wrong sides together, stitch a ⅜in (1cm) seam along the long edge of the larger tie piece and one edge on the knot. Trim the seams to ¼in (6mm) and press them to one side, positioning them in the centre of each piece.

33 With the seam on the inside, fold the larger piece in half widthways and stitch together the short edges, allowing a ⅜in (1cm) seam. Trim the seam to ¼in (6mm) and press to one side, positioning the seam at the centre back.

34 Turn and press ¼in (6mm) towards the seam at each short end of the knot. With the seam on the inside, wrap the knot around the middle of the larger piece to form a bow shape. Slipstitch each pressed edge to the larger piece of the bow tie, sewing each side so they meet at the back.

35 Position the bow tie on the doll's shirt so the top edge is in line with the seam at the neck. Turn back each side of the bow and stitch the knot securely to the body on each side.

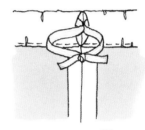

31

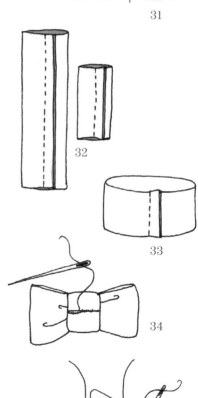

32

33

34

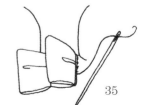

35

127

aviator-style hat

This classic hat is in a simple, practical style that will suit a little boy or a girl. It is fully lined and securely fastens under the chin with a buckle.

The following guide shows how much material you will need for an average-sized child.

FABRIC WIDTH (WITHOUT NAP)	ONE SIZE TO FIT 1–3 YEARS
36in (90cm)	Main fabric: ¹/₂yd (0.45m) Lining: ¹/₂yd (0.45m)
45in (115cm)	Main fabric: ¹/₂yd (0.45m) Lining: ¹/₂yd (0.45m)
60in (150cm)	Main fabric: ¹/₂yd (0.45m) Lining: ¹/₂yd (0.45m)

Suggested fabrics

Cotton, linen, denim
Lining: cotton, cotton blend

Sewing notions

- Thread to match main fabric and lining
- Small buckle with an interior width of ¾in (2cm)

Pattern pieces on sheet F

90 Side head (cut 2 in main fabric, cut 2 in lining fabric)
91 Top head (cut 1 in main fabric, cut 1 in lining fabric)
92 Chin strap (cut 1 in main fabric)
93 Buckle loop (cut 1 in main fabric)

Seam allowances

Take ³/₈in (1cm) seam allowances throughout, unless otherwise stated.

Finished size

To fit 1–3 years, up to 19¾in (50cm) head circumference

36in (90cm), 45in (115cm) and 60in (150cm) wide – MAIN FABRIC

SELVEDGES

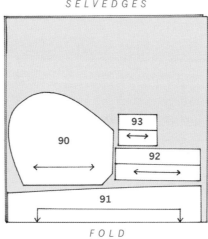

FOLD

Open out fabric to cut chin strap and buckle loop

36in (90cm), 45in (115cm) and 60in (150cm) wide – LINING

SELVEDGES

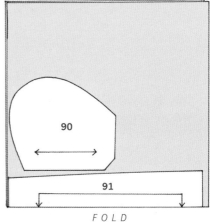

FOLD

Key
☐ *Right side of fabric*
▨ *Wrong side of fabric*

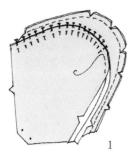

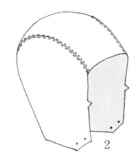

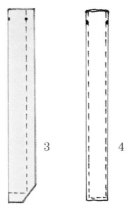

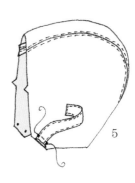

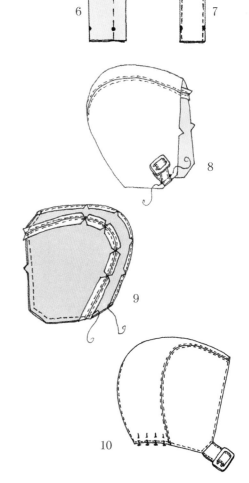

Instructions

1 With right sides of main fabric pieces together, matching notches, pin the sides to the top piece. Insert plenty of pins to ease the fabric of the top of the hat around the curves of the sides. Stitch together, allowing ⅜in (1cm) seam. Notch the curves and press the seams open *(see page 153)*.

2 Topstitch *(see page 151)* along each side of the seams.

Strap

3 With right sides together, fold the chin strap at the line indicated on the pattern and stitch the edges, allowing a ⅜in (1cm) seam and leaving one short end open. Trim the seam and cut diagonally into the corner, taking care not to cut into the stitching.

4 Turn the strap right side out and press. Topstitch close to the edges.

5 On the outside of the hat, matching the dots, tack the chin strap in position on the left-hand side, aligning the raw edges.

6 With right sides together, fold the buckle loop at the line indicated on the pattern and stitch the long edge, allowing a ⅜in (1cm) seam.

7 Turn the buckle loop right-side out and press. Topstitch close to the edges.

8 Thread the buckle loop through the buckle and fold in half widthways. Tack the loop in position on the right-hand side of the hat, matching the dots and aligning the raw edges.

Lining

9 Follow Step 1 to join the top and side lining pieces. With right sides together, matching notches and seams, pin the main hat to the lining, sandwiching the strap and buckle loop between the layers. Stitch around the outside edges, allowing a ⅜in (1cm) seam and leaving an opening of around 2¾in (7cm) at the back neck.

10 Turn right side out and push the lining inside the hat. Press the hat, turning under the edges of the opening at the back of the neck. Pin the pressed edges of the opening together. Topstitch all around the outside edges.

bib

The bib is a simple project that doesn't use much fabric. It is an ideal way to upcycle old clothing and create a small but perfect gift.

Fabric required
½ x ⅓yd (0.45 x 0.3m) each of main fabric and facing

Suggested fabrics
Light- to medium-weight fabrics, quilting cotton, shirting, linen, towelling

Sewing notions
• Thread to match fabric
• 1 x ⅜in (1cm) snap fastener
For the appliqué
• Fusible web interfacing
• Remnants of fabric

Seam allowances
Take ⅜in (1cm) seam allowances throughout, unless otherwise stated

Finished measurements
One size to fit 6 months–2 years
Length of bib front from neck:
5¾in (14.5cm)
Width:
8in (20.5cm) at widest part

Pattern note
Reverse the pattern to cut the facing.

Pattern piece on sheet E
94 Bib (cut 1 in main fabric,
     cut 1 in facing fabric)
Templates for stars, pear and leaf are found on page 168.

Key
☐ Right side of fabric
☐ Wrong side of fabric

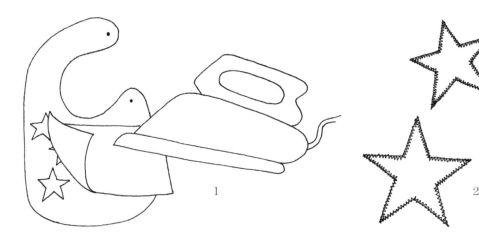

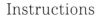

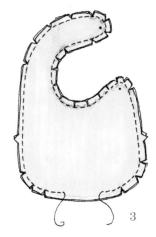

Instructions

Appliqué

1   Trace the template of the stars or the pear and leaf from the bib pattern onto the paper side of the fusible web interfacing. Following the manufacturer's instructions, apply the fusible web interfacing to the back of the chosen fabrics *(see page 145)*. Cut out the shapes and position the appliqué on the right side of the bib, as indicated on the pattern. Use a damp pressing cloth under the iron when fusing the shapes to the bib.

2   Use a narrow zigzag machine stitch or hand-embroidered buttonhole stitch to finish the edges *(see pages 151 and 167)*.

Attach facing

3   With right sides together, matching notches, stitch the front to the facing, allowing a ⅜in (1cm) seam and leaving an opening of around 2in (5cm) at the lower edge. Notch the outward curves and snip the inward curves *(see page 153)*.

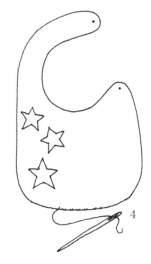

4   Turn right side out and press. Slipstitch *(see page 151)* the opening closed.

Finishing off

5   Sew a snap fastener at the dots indicated on the pattern *(see page 165)*.

play apron

A large pocket is divided into sections to hold treasures such as paintbrushes or a small drawing book. The edges are bound and buttons fasten the apron at the back of the neck.

The following guide shows how much material you will need for an average-sized child.

FABRIC WIDTH (WITHOUT NAP)	1 YEAR OLD	2 YEAR OLD	3 YEAR OLD
36in (90cm)	Main fabric: ⅞yd (0.8m)	Main fabric: ⅞yd (0.8m)	Main fabric: ⅞yd (0.8m)
45in (115cm)	Main fabric: ⅞yd (0.8m)	Main fabric: ⅞yd (0.8m)	Main fabric: ⅞yd (0.8m)
60in (150cm)	Main fabric: ⅞yd (0.8m)	Main fabric: ⅞yd (0.8m)	Main fabric: ⅞yd (0.8m)

For the binding
½ x ½yd (0.45 x 0.45m) of contrast fabric

Suggested fabrics
Linen, denim, calico

Sewing notions
- Thread to match fabric
- 2 x ⅝in (1.5cm) buttons

Seam allowances
Take ⅝in (1.5cm) seam allowances on side and shoulder seams and ⅜in (1cm) seam allowances on bound edges.

Finished measurements
Back length:
1 year: 19in (48.5cm)
2 years: 20in (51cm)
3 years: 21in (53.5cm)

Pattern pieces on sheet D
95 Front (cut 1 in main fabric)
96 Back (cut 2 in main fabric)
97 Pocket (cut 2 in main fabric)

36in (90cm), 45in (115cm) and 60in (150cm) wide

SELVEDGES

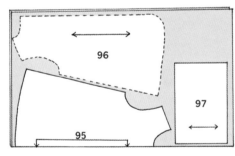

FOLD

Broken lines indicate reverse side of pattern

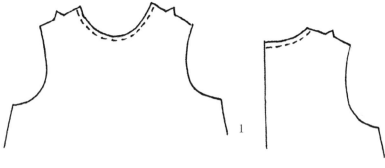

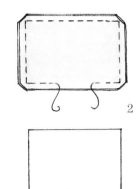

1

2

Instructions

1   Staystitch *(see page 151)* the neck edges of the backs and front at the ⅜in (1cm) seam allowance.

Pocket

2   With right sides together, pin and stitch around the pocket, leaving an opening of around 2¾in (7cm) at the lower edge. Trim the seam and cut diagonally across the corners, taking care not to cut the stitching. Turn the pocket right side out and press well. Slipstitch the opening closed *(see page 151)*.

3   On the outside of the apron front, pin the pocket in position, matching the small dots. Topstitch *(see page 151)* close to the side and lower edges. Run a line of stitches along each broken line indicated on the pattern to divide the pocket into sections.

Join front to back pieces

4   With right sides together, stitch the front to the back at the shoulders and side seams. Press seams open.

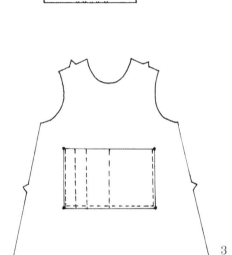

3

Key

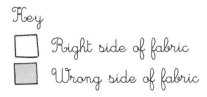
Right side of fabric
Wrong side of fabric

4

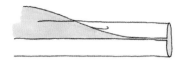

5

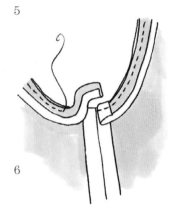

6

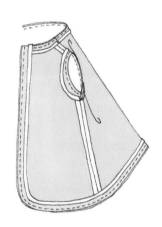

7

8

Binding

5   Cut 1½in (4cm)-wide bias strips from the contrast fabric and sew the short edges together to make the binding *(see page 160)*. Press a ⅜in (1cm) seam allowance along each long edge.

6   To bind the armholes, open out one pressed edge of the binding. Turn under ⅜in (1cm) at the short end and, with the right side of the binding to the inside of the garment, align the turned edge with the underarm seam. Pin and stitch the edge of the binding to the ⅜in (1cm) seam allowance of the armhole, overlapping the binding at the end before cutting away the excess.

7   Turn under ⅜in (1cm) at the short end of the binding. Starting at the shoulder seam, with the right side of the binding to the inside of the garment, pin and stitch the creased edge of the binding to a ⅜in (1cm) seam allowance at the edges of the apron, overlapping the end and folding out the fullness of the binding at the corners *(see page 161)*. Press the seam towards the binding.

8   Turn the binding around the apron edges and armholes to the right side of the garment to encase the seam allowances. Pin the pressed edges over the seams and topstitch close to the pressed edges, pivoting the needle at the corners. Press the bound edges.

Finishing off

9   Finish by working two buttonholes by hand or machine *(see page 163)* on the right back as indicated on the pattern. Lap the right back over the left, matching the centre back. Mark the position of the buttons to correspond with the buttonholes. Attach the buttons to the left back *(see page 165)*.

9

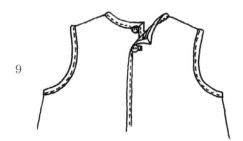

baby boots & shoes

Here is the perfect finishing touch to an outfit.
A pair of little lace-up boots or Mary-Jane shoes can
be made to match everything in a baby's wardrobe.

Fabric required
¼yd (0.2m) each in main fabric
and lining fabric

Suggested fabrics
Medium-weight cotton, wool, linen

Sewing notions
- Thread to match fabric
For the lace-up boots
- 2 x 20in (51cm) lengths of ¼–⅜in
  (6mm–1cm)-wide ribbon
- 8 x ¼in (6mm) eyelets
For the Mary-Jane shoes
- Lightweight iron-on interfacing the
  size of one ankle strap cut in half
  lengthways
- 2 x ⅜in (1cm) buttons

Finished size
Approximate shoe length:
0–3 months: 4in (10cm)
3–6 months: 4⅜in (11cm)
6–12 months: 5in (13cm)

Pattern pieces on sheet A
98 Lace-up boot back (cut 2 in main
    fabric, cut 2 in lining fabric)
99 Lace-up boot front (cut 2 in main
    fabric, cut 2 in lining fabric)
100 Shoe and boot sole (cut 2 in main
    fabric, cut 2 in lining fabric)
101 Mary-Jane shoe (cut 2 in main
    fabric, cut 2 in lining fabric)
102 Mary-Jane shoe strap
    (cut 2 in main fabric)

Seam allowances
Take ⅜in (1cm) seam allowances
throughout, unless otherwise stated.

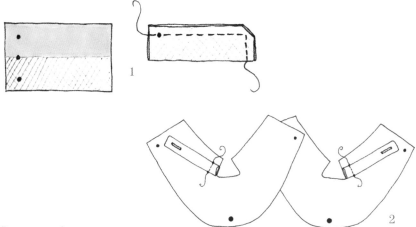

Instructions

Mary-Jane shoes

1 Following the manufacturer's instructions, apply iron-on
   interfacing *(see page 145)* up to the fold line on the
   wrong side of the straps. With right sides together, fold
   the straps lengthways along the line indicated on the
   pattern. Stitch a ⅜in (1cm) seam along the long edge
   and one short end of the strap. Trim the seams and cut
   diagonally across the corners, taking care not to cut into
   the stitching.

2 Turn right side out and press. Work a buttonhole by
   hand or machine on each strap, as indicated on the
   pattern *(see page 163)*. With the seams facing towards
   the lower edge of the shoe, tack the straps in place
   on the right side of the upper linings, matching the
   small dots. Remember to place them on opposite sides
   to make a matching pair of shoes.

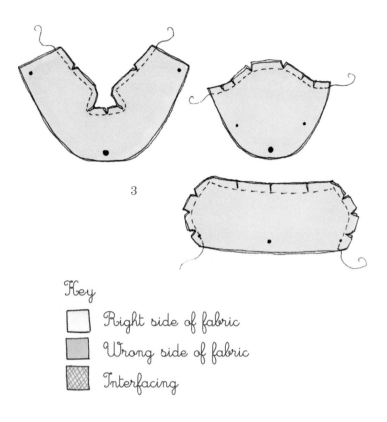

3

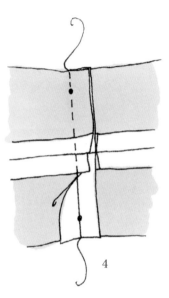

4

Key

 Right side of fabric

Wrong side of fabric

Interfacing

Boots and shoes

3   With right sides together, stitch uppers and upper
linings together, leaving the lower edges open. Trim the
seam, notch the outward curves, snip the inward curves
(see page 153) and cut diagonally across the corners,
taking care not to cut into the stitching. Turn right side
out and press.

Mary-Jane shoes

4   With right sides together, matching the seams, stitch
all the way down the back seam of the shoe uppers
and linings. Press the seam open. Turn the shoe uppers
right side out and press.

Lace-up boots

5   Aligning the raw edges, place the side back over the
tongue and pin in place, matching the small dots.

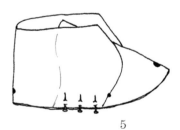

5

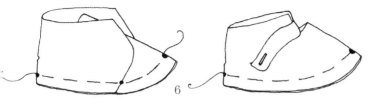

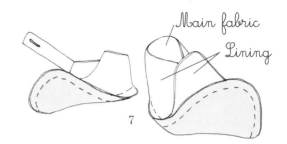

Main fabric

Lining

7

Boots and shoes

6   With wrong sides together, tack the lower edges of the uppers and linings together.

7   With right sides together, matching the large dots at the front and the medium dots at the back, stitch the sole to the upper.

8   With right sides together, matching the dots and with the uppers sandwiched in between, pin the sole lining to the sole. Insert plenty of pins to ease the fabric and keep the upper away from the edges so it does not get caught in the stitches. Stitch through all layers, leaving a 2in (5cm) opening on one side to turn the boot or shoe. Trim the seam and notch the curves.

Finishing off

9   Turn right side out and slipstitch *(see page 151)* the opening in the lining to close. Push the lining inside the boot or shoe. Following the manufacturer's instructions, attach the eyelets to each side of the boot, as indicated on the pattern. Thread the ribbon through to fasten and trim the ends. Sew a button to the side of each shoe *(see page 165)*, as indicated by an 'X' on the pattern, to fasten the strap.

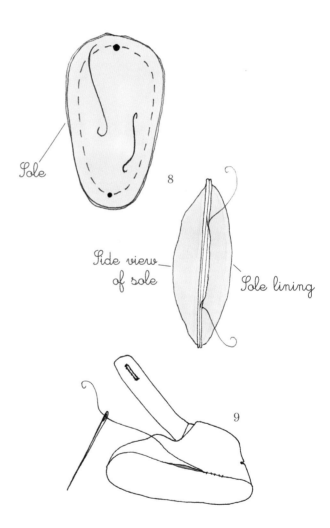

Sole

8

Side view of sole

Sole lining

9

Techniques

Simple steps that show you
how to create quick and
professional-looking results.

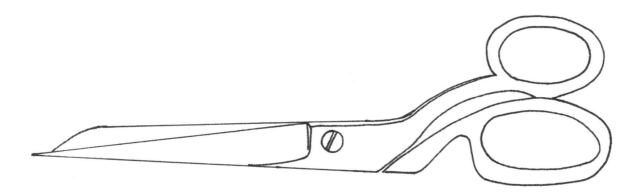

sewing tools

A basic knowledge of needlework and a few essential tools are all that are needed to produce a beautiful handmade garment or accessory for a baby or toddler.

Scissors

Tailor's and dressmaking shears have long blades and a bent handle so the scissors can rest on the table while cutting, keeping the fabric flat. The blades should be kept sharp for ease of cutting. They must be kept solely for cutting fabric and a separate pair of scissors used for cutting paper patterns.

A small pair of very sharp, pointed scissors is essential for cutting threads and can also be useful for fiddly tasks such as unpicking stitches.

Buttonhole scissors are useful because they are made specifically for the job, with short, sharp pointed blades to cut the fabric. They often have an adjustable screw so that the buttonhole can be cut to the size required.

Pinking shears can be used for finishing seams; the jagged blades cut a zigzag line that prevents the fabric from fraying. They should be kept for fabric only because cutting paper will blunt the blades.

Marking tools

Tailor's chalk

Tailor's chalk is used for marking pattern shapes on fabric and can be brushed away. It comes in white for use on dark cloth and in various colours for use on light fabric. It should be kept sharp to produce a clean line. The chalk can also be found in the form of a pencil.

Tracing wheel

A tracing wheel is mainly used for marking and duplicating lines on paper patterns and transferring pattern lines to fabric. It has a finely spiked wheel with very sharp points that will not tear the paper. The wheels should not be used on silks because the spikes can tear the fine threads of the fabric.

Carbon paper

Dressmaker's carbon paper is used in the same way as the stationery kind, for copying documents. It is heavier, making it easy to pin to a fabric without tearing, and is available in yellow, white, blue and red, to work with light and dark fabrics.

Pins

Pins come in various sizes, for use on fine laces to heavy woven cloth; ones with coloured glass heads are easy to find in fabric. Take care not to use pins that are rusty or blunt – they will damage the fabric.

Tape measure

A tape measure is a vital piece of equipment for dressmaking. A PVC tape is preferable, as it won't stretch or tear like a fabric or paper one.

Thimble

The thimble should fit comfortably, without falling off, protecting the finger that pushes the needle through the fabric.

Beeswax

Beeswax is used for strengthening thread and preventing knots when working buttonholes or inserting zips by hand. It also helps when threading needles. Draw the thread across the beeswax a couple of times to coat it.

Needles

Needles are available in an array of sizes for a multitude of needlework tasks. Make sure they are not rusty and the points are sharp so as not to damage the fabric. The needle should go through the fabric with ease, without leaving a mark or hole.

Hand-stitching needles

Sharps are used for general sewing and come in various sizes to suit different weights of fabric. They have a relatively large eye to facilitate threading. Betweens are short, slim needles with a narrow eye, ideal for working small, even stitches. There are also needles specifically for darning, embroidery, quilting, beading and millinery.

MACHINE NEEDLE SIZE GUIDE

Size	Fabric examples
8/60	Sheer fabrics, chiffon, georgette
10/70	Lining fabrics, cotton lawn
11/80	Shirting fabrics, lightweight cotton
14/90	Cotton sateen, linen
16/100	Denim, canvas
18/110	Leather, vinyl, upholstery fabrics

Machine needles

It is important to use the right needle size for the weight of fabric to produce the best results. Universal needles have a slightly rounded point for use with knitted fabrics but they are sharp enough to go through woven fabrics. For knitted fabrics, a ballpoint needle slips between the fibres of the fabric, preventing snagging. There are also needles specifically for use with denim and leather, and twin needles, used for working two even rows of stitching.

Needle sizes are shown in both imperial and metric. The smallest sizes relate to the finer needles for use with lightweight fabrics. Where the number is larger, the needle is bigger, for sewing medium- to heavy-weight material.

Sewing machines

Many modern sewing machines have a huge variety of stitch selections. However, all the projects in this book can easily be made with a fairly basic machine that does straight and zigzag stitch. A lot of machines offer automatic buttonholing, which is very useful, but not vital. Even an old treadle or hand-operated sewing machine can be used, and if the zigzag stitch is not available, the buttonholes can be worked by hand *(see page 163)*.

Care of the machine

Regular maintenance of your sewing machine is essential to keep it running smoothly. Always unplug it before cleaning and oiling.

Lint (fabric and thread particles) gets caught up near the bobbin and in hidden areas, so should be removed before it causes problems.

Use proper sewing-machine oil and refer to the manual for the areas that need it. Tighten all the screws and then work some machine stitches on scraps of fabric to catch any excess oil.

Using the machine

Have your machine set up at an area with plenty of light and where you can be comfortably seated. Before sewing, make sure that the machine is threaded correctly and that the two threads, from the needle and bobbin, are placed towards the back of the work. Turn the wheel towards you so that the needle is in the work, preventing a tangle of threads. Every time you begin a new project or use a different type of stitch, practise first on a spare piece of fabric to check the tension and avoid having to unpick mistakes. Taking it slowly will ensure control of the machine and problems with the tension or tangling threads will be less likely.

fabric & threads

Natural fabric originates from animals, vegetables or minerals while synthetic fabric is artificially produced from chemical compounds. When choosing a fabric, select soft, natural fibres that won't irritate sensitive skin.

Wool

Wool is a softly woven, comfortable and functional fabric. Felted wool is produced by matting the fibres together using heat, moisture and pressure. A felted wool mix was used to make the cape on page 94.

Silk

Silk is very luxurious with a strong natural fibre. It is produced from the cocoons spun by the Bombyx mori moth lava (silkworm). A remnant of silk charmeuse was used to make the sash for the party dress on page 88, making it extra special.

Cotton

Cotton is very practical and resilient. It can be woven into very fine, sheer fabrics such as organdie and voile. It can also produce durable materials, including canvas and denim. Cotton has been used for many of the projects in this book, including the main fabric and lining for the rompers on page 58.

Linen

Linen is made from flax-plant fibres. A strong fabric, it has natural irregularities in the weave. It is cool and comfortable although it does tend to crease easily. Various projects were made using linen, including the play apron on page 132.

Tulle

Polyester spotted tulle was used for the overskirt on the party dress, page 88. Tulle is a net with a hexagonal mesh. Made from silk and cotton as well as synthetic fibres, it is used for bridal veils and ballet tutus.

PUL fabric

PUL fabric is a washable, 100% polyester knit fabric, backed with a polyurethane laminate. To sew it, use a walking foot, which feeds the fabric through as it is stitched, or lay a strip of wax paper over the PUL fabric when sewing and tear it away when the seam is finished. Pin inside the seam allowance to prevent making holes in the fabric and use a ballpoint needle. PUL fabric was used for the rain hat on page 118.

Threads

When finding thread to match the fabric, choose one that is slightly darker on the reel because it will look lighter when worked into the fabric. Use a strong thread for sewing seams. Polyester thread is strong and suitable for hand and machine sewing on all fabrics.

Tacking thread is cheaper and since the stitches are temporary, will break easily – perfect for the task, but not good for sewing permanent seams. Use a contrast colour for tacking so the stitches are easy to see when they need to be removed.

Embroidery threads are available in a wide range of shades, and the strands can be divided to produce finer stitches.

When sewing on the machine, use the same thread on the bobbin as in the needle. If you are stitching a dark binding to a light fabric, such as in the tabard project on page 109, the colour on the bobbin and needle can be changed to match, but don't mix the fibres.

A rain hat in a bright polka-dot print PUL fabric will cheer up rainy days.

The felted fabric for the cape is a blend of 80% wool and 20% polyamide.

A layer of tulle and a silk sash make this dress perfect for special occasions.

Striped, crisp cotton shirting fabric for the smart, long-sleeved shirt.

Lightweight linen is ideal for a cool short-sleeved shirt.

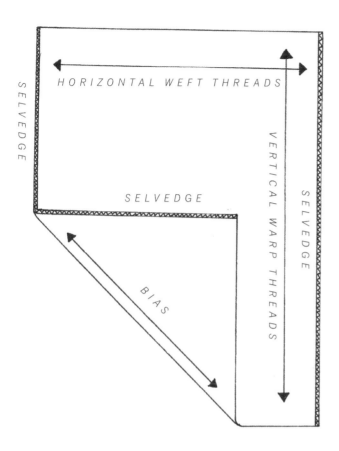

SELVEDGE

HORIZONTAL WEFT THREADS

SELVEDGE

VERTICAL WARP THREADS

SELVEDGE

BIAS

Preparing fabric

Launder washable fabrics before use so that any shrinkage occurs before the item is made up. Press the fabric before you cut out the pattern, making sure the iron is set to the right heat for the fabric type. The direction of the grain will affect the way the finished garment hangs, so it is very important that the grain of the fabric is straight before you start a project. The warp and weft (vertical and horizontal) threads should be at right angles to each other.

Straightening the fabric

Straighten up the weft edges (the horizontal threads that lie between the selvedges) by clipping the fabric at a selvedge edge and tearing it across, or by withdrawing a thread from the fabric and cutting along the straight line it produces. Straighten the fabric by stretching on the bias or crossway until the edges lie together.

Interfacing

Interfacing adds structure to an area of a garment, such as a collar or lapel. It is available in light-, medium- or heavy-weight, to match the weight of the fabric you are using. Interfacing comes in black or charcoal grey for dark fabrics and white for light fabrics.

Woven interfacing has a grain that should be matched with the grain of the fabric that is to be interfaced.

Non-woven interfacing can be cut in any direction as it has no grain, making it more economical than woven interfacing. Knitted interfacing is available for use with stretch fabrics. The two main types of interfacing are sew-in and iron-on.

Sew-in interfacing

This is stitched to the fabric and produces a soft drape. It is also used on fabrics that are heat-sensitive or open-weave and unsuitable for iron-on interfacing.

Iron-on interfacing

Iron-on interfacing has a shiny, fusible side, which is laid on top of the wrong side of the fabric. It is a good idea to test it out on a scrap of material first to check the weight you are using is correct. Make sure that the iron is at the right temperature for the fabric. Place a damp cloth over the pieces and press the iron down for a few seconds, then lift and repeat on another area. Do not drag the iron over the fabric, as it could pucker or move the material. After the interfacing has been fused in place, allow the fabric to cool before stitching.

Fusible web interfacing

This is a double-sided fusible interfacing and is used to bond two pieces of fabric together. It is ideal for appliqué *(see page 166)*.

understanding patterns

Use the information given on the patterns and transfer all the essential markings to the prepared fabric before you begin to sew.

Pattern markings

The diagrams on a pattern show how it is to be laid on the fabric and where the cutting lines are, as well as features such as the position of pockets and buttonholes.

Buttonhole

The positions of the buttonholes are marked on the pattern by solid lines with a bar at each end. The length of the line is the correct length of the buttonhole required for the size of button given in the list of notions at the beginning of each project.

Centre front and centre back

The central line that runs vertically down the front or back is given as CF for the centre front and CB for the centre back.

Cutting line

The cutting line is a continuous line on the pattern. The seam allowances are given on the pattern pieces as well as in the instructions for each project.

Sewing line

A broken line on a pattern, such as the play apron, on sheet D, indicates the sewing line.

Grain lines

When laying out the pattern on the fabric, make sure that the line of the grain, which is marked by a long, double-ended arrow, follows the selvedge of the fabric. Some pattern pieces need to be placed on a fold, which is indicated by the arrows at an angle to the grain line. Fold the fabric so the selvedges are parallel and place the fold line on the pattern against that of the fabric.

Notches and dots

The notches are used to match the seams accurately when they are sewn together. Where there are two or more notches together on a pattern, cut them in blocks for ease, rather than individually. Match the notches with those of the same number on the piece to be joined. Dots refer to points that should meet on pattern pieces or show where a line of stitching should begin or end.

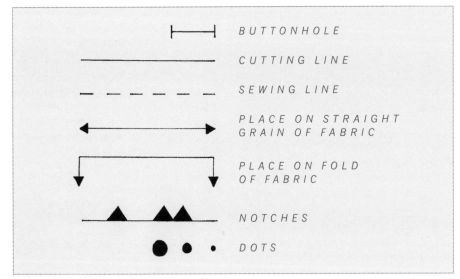

BUTTONHOLE

CUTTING LINE

SEWING LINE

PLACE ON STRAIGHT GRAIN OF FABRIC

PLACE ON FOLD OF FABRIC

NOTCHES

DOTS

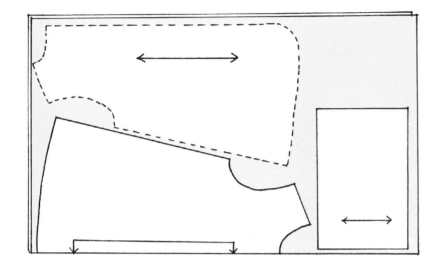

Broken lines in the cutting layout indicate the reverse side of the pattern piece.

Place the pattern with the right side facing down on the fabric.

Laying out the pattern

Where applicable, follow the cutting layout for the width of the fabric you have chosen. This appears at the beginning of a project. Each pattern piece is numbered so it can be easily identified on the cutting layouts. The broken lines indicate the reverse side of the pattern pieces, so should be placed with the right side facing down on the fabric. Where the lines of the pattern pieces in the cutting layouts are continuous, these should be placed right side up on the fabric.

For double thickness, fold the fabric with right sides together and lay the pattern pieces on the wrong side. For single thickness, lay the pattern pieces on the right side of the fabric. When more than one of the same piece is to be cut one at a time, reverse the paper pattern for the second piece.

Nap

The nap is a pile produced by directional raised fibres on fabrics such as velvet. Fabrics with a pile or a one-way pattern must be cut with all the pattern pieces placed facing the same direction. The yardage/meterage required in this book is for fabrics without nap, so you should allow for extra if you choose a fabric with nap or a one-way design. When working with a nap, the pattern should be pinned to the wrong side of the fabric before cutting.

The direction of the pile can be found by brushing your hand over the material. Brushing with the direction of the nap will feel smooth, whereas brushing against the nap will feel rough. A shiny, silky look is produced when the nap is running down. When the nap is running up, the fabric shade is deeper and richer.

Cutting out the pattern pieces

Pin the pattern pieces to the fabric so the pins lay in the same direction and do not obstruct the cutting line. Use enough pins to hold the pattern down, taking care not to pucker the fabric. Using sharp scissors, place one hand flat on the pattern and fabric to hold it down, keeping it flat so the lines being cut are accurate. Cut away from you along the seam line, the solid lines of the pattern. Cut notches outwards, rather than into the seam allowance.

Key

☐ *Right side of fabric*
▨ *Wrong side of fabric*

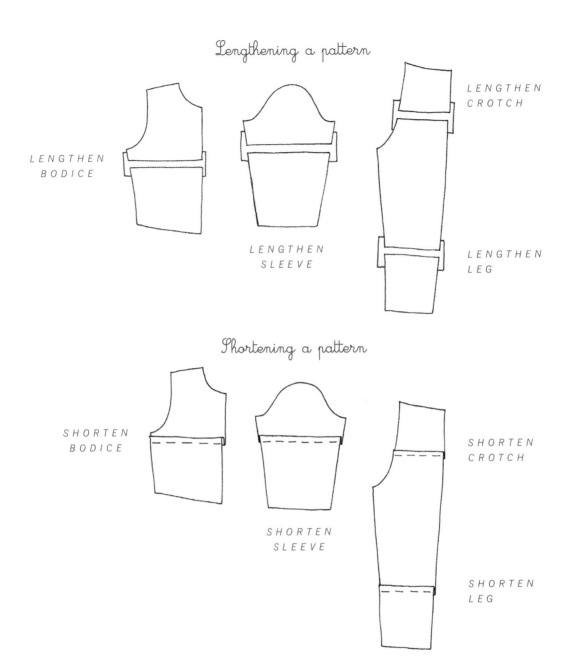

Lengthening a pattern

LENGTHEN
BODICE

LENGTHEN
SLEEVE

LENGTHEN
CROTCH

LENGTHEN
LEG

Shortening a pattern

SHORTEN
BODICE

SHORTEN
SLEEVE

SHORTEN
CROTCH

SHORTEN
LEG

Adjusting a pattern

Check that the measurements given for the pattern you are using correspond with the child's size. If not, you'll need to lengthen or shorten the pattern.

Lengthening a pattern

Cut the pattern across the width and place paper behind the pieces. Adjust the pieces so that they are even and are the required distance apart. Stick the pieces to the paper behind with masking tape or sticky tape. Trim the excess paper from each side.

Shortening a pattern

Fold the pattern across the width and overlap the pieces evenly to take up the surplus length required.

pattern sheets

Each pattern piece is numbered so it can be easily identified from the list given at the beginning of each project, as well as making it easy to follow the cutting layouts provided.

Using the pattern sheets

Select the pattern pieces for the project you are making. These are listed at the beginning of each project and can be found on the pattern sheets at the back of the book. Each sheet has been given a letter for easy reference. The pattern pieces for each particular project are colour-coded and each individual piece is numbered. For example, the cape's pattern pieces (*see page 94*), are found on pattern sheet B and are numbered 51–55.

Copying the patterns

The pattern pieces on the enclosed pattern sheets are printed at actual size, ready to be copied. The patterns can be traced using dressmaker's tissue paper or tracing paper, available in rolls. Another way to copy the patterns is by taking them to a copy shop to be printed. They can also be photocopied at home, although some of these pieces may need to be taped together if they are larger than your copier paper size. Make sure the patterns are laid flat so they don't distort when printed. Check you have every pattern piece required before you start the project and that you have transferred all the pattern markings (*see page 146*), ready to use.

Cutting out the right size

The garment patterns are in various sizes, ranging from 0 to 3 years. To calculate the size you need, refer to page 171 for how to take children's measurements and, based on those figures, choose which will be the correct size of pattern to cut out. If the child is between sizes, cut out the pattern in the larger size. Each size is labelled along the cutting lines. When tracing or cutting the photocopied pattern pieces, follow the lines according to the size you require.

stitches

A variety of hand and machine stitches are used throughout this book, to create beautiful handmade garments or adorable accessories for a baby or toddler.

Hand stitches

Hand stitches are usually worked from right to left. To secure the end of the thread to the fabric, work a few stitches over each other at the beginning. Alternatively, knot the end of the thread and insert the needle from the wrong side of the fabric.

Catch stitch

This stitch is worked from left to right and holds fabric in place, protecting the raw edge at the same time. It is used for the cape on page 94.

Starting at the left-hand side, work a small horizontal stitch near the edge of the top layer of fabric. Bring the needle to the right of the stitch and work another small stitch in the lower layer of fabric, just by the edge of the top layer, creating a diagonal stitch. Make stitches in the top and lower layers of fabric alternately to produce a zigzag effect.

Prick stitch

The prick stitch is used to insert the zip in the party dress on page 88.

Bring the needle through to the right side of the fabric. Insert the needle right behind the point where it first emerged, carrying it back by just one or two threads of fabric and bring it back up around ¼in (6mm) from the previous stitch. Continue in this way to produce a row of tiny stitches on the surface and longer, reinforcing stitches beneath.

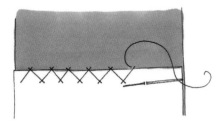

Catch stitch

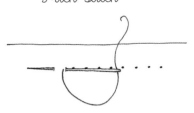

Prick stitch

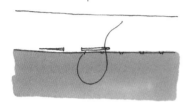

Slipstitch

Tacking stitch

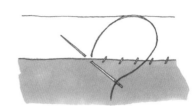

Hem stitch

Slipstitch

This stitch produces an almost invisible finish, used for hemming and attaching trimmings. Pass the needle through the folded edge and, at the same point, pick up a thread or two of the fabric underneath. Continue in this way, spacing the stitches evenly around ⅛–¼in (3–6mm) apart.

Tacking stitch

This is a temporary stitch used to join pieces of fabric ready for fitting and permanent stitching. It is the easiest and quickest hand-sewing stitch. Knot the end of the thread and work large stitches from right to left. Finish with a couple of stitches worked over each other to secure the end. When the seam has been permanently sewn by machine or hand, remove the tacking stitches.

Hem stitch

Bring the thread through to the edge of the folded hem. Pick up a thread of fabric and pass the needle diagonally through the edge of the hem. Continue in this way, spacing the stitches around ¼in (6mm) apart.

Machine stitches

Staystitching

This is a straight machine stitch used around curved and angled edges, such as necklines, to prevent stretching when handling before joining pieces together. The stitching is done ⅛in (3mm) inside the seam line. The stitches do not need to be removed because they will be hidden between the seam allowance and the edge inside the finished garment.

Zigzag stitch

The zigzag stitch is available on most sewing machines, though the very old machines often only do straight stitching. Zigzag can be used as a decorative stitch with a contrasting thread, or for finishing raw edges and, by adjusting the length and width of the stitch, will make a neat buttonhole.

Topstitching

Topstitching

This is a line of straight machine stitching worked on the right side of the fabric, parallel to seams and edges. It is used as both a decorative and a functional stitch.

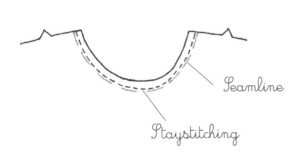

Seamline

Staystitching

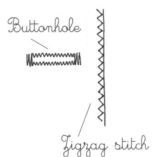

Buttonhole

Zigzag stitch

seams

A seam produces the structure and shape required to create a three-dimensional form from the cut pieces of fabric. Taking care over finishing the seams will produce a more professional-looking and durable item.

Pinning seams

Pinning and tacking seams is very useful if you are a beginner, ensuring the fabric will not slip about when stitching, so producing a neat seam and avoiding mistakes. As your confidence builds with experience, you may feel you no longer need to pin seams before you stitch.

Pinning fabric along the seam line

Insert the pins so that the points face away from you. As the pins cannot be stitched over when in line with the needle, they will be easy to remove with the pin heads facing towards you; you will also avoid pricking your finger.

Stitching over pins

Pins can be machine stitched over when they are at right angles to the edge of the work. This way, the needle will not get broken by hitting the pins and they can be removed after stitching the seam. This is a particularly useful method to use when easing the fullness of fabric.

Flat seam

The patterns in this book use a flat seam unless otherwise stated.

With right sides of fabric together, stitch along the ⅝in (1.5cm) seam line and press the seam open. To secure the line of stitching and prevent the stitches from unravelling, run the machine backwards and then forwards over the first and last few stitches. The raw edges of the seam can be trimmed to neaten it.

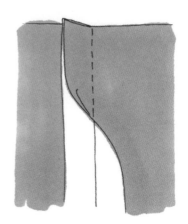

Flat seam

Pinning fabric along the seamline

Stitching over pins

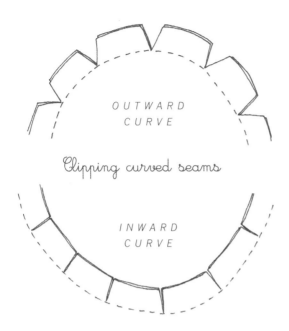

Clipping curved seams

OUTWARD CURVE

INWARD CURVE

Clipping seams

Where a seam is curved, snipping or cutting notches into the fabric will enable it to lie flat. On fabrics that fray easily, cut the layers of the seams separately and make sure the snips and notches of each seam do not match. To reduce bulk in heavier fabrics, seams can be layered so they lay flat by cutting each layer of the seam slightly smaller than the last.

Clipping curved seams

For those that curve outwards, cut a V-shape into the seam close to the stitch line. For inward curves, snip a straight line in the seam close to the stitches.

Trimming corners

Corners should be trimmed to an angle so the fabric lies flat when the work is turned right side out. An inverted corner should be snipped close to the seam line.

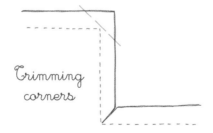

Trimming corners

Seam finishes

Finishing the seams will neaten the garment and prevent fraying, therefore making it more durable. All the seams on the projects in this book should be finished as they are stitched, by using any of the following methods:

Turned edge

Turn under the raw edges of the seam and stitch close to the fold.

Zigzag finish

Work a line of zigzag stitches close to the raw edges of the seam. Practise on a scrap of fabric beforehand to achieve the desired stitch length and width.

Turned edge

Zigzag finish

Special seams

The raw edges of the following seams do not need any finishing. These seams are both neat and hardwearing and will withstand regular laundering.

Fell seam

The stitching forms a decorative seam that is visible on the right side of the fabric. It is used for lingerie but also suitable for heavier garments, such as jeans and outerwear.

1 With wrong sides of fabric together, stitch along the ⅝in (1.5cm) seam line and press it to one side.

2 Trim the lower-edge seam allowance to ⅛in (3mm). Turn under and press ¼in (6mm) on the raw edge of the other seam allowance.

3 Press the wider seam allowance over the narrow, trimmed edge and stitch down, close to the fold, encasing the raw edge. This seam is finished on the right side of the fabric. Where the seam is curved, a French seam is more suitable.

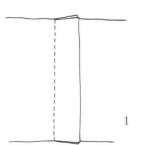 1

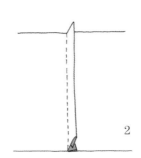 2

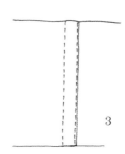 3

French seam

Where the pattern states that the right sides of the fabric should be together to sew the seam, start a French seam with the wrong sides of the fabric together.

1 Stitch the first seam with wrong sides together, working ¼in (6mm) from the seam line.

2 Press the seam to one side, then turn the work to the inside and press.

3 With right sides together, stitch along the seam allowance to encase the first seam. When a French seam is stitched on a curved line, snip the first seam to allow it to expand around the curve so that it sits flat inside the second line of stitches *(see page 153)*.

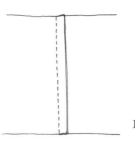 1

 2

 3

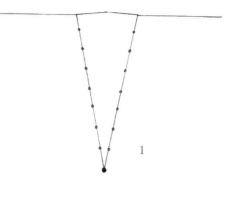

1

2

Darts

Darts create the shaping by controlling the fullness in the fabric to fit the garment smoothly over the contours of the body.

3

1   Before removing the paper pattern from the cut-out fabric piece, make small holes in the pattern paper at the pointed end and along the lines of the dart. Mark the position of the dart on the fabric with a tailor's chalk pencil.

2   With right sides together, fold the centre of the dart, matching the lines on each side. Stitch carefully from the wide end, tapering off to the point. Vertical darts should be pressed towards the centre front or centre back, and horizontal darts should be pressed towards the hem of the garment.

3   To reduce bulk in heavy-weight fabric, slash to within ½in (1.25cm) of the point of the dart and press open.

gathering

Gathering is a simple method to adjust fullness in the fabric and to ease seams, such as on the head of a sleeve.

Gathering by hand or machine

Straight rows of running stitches are used to gather fabric by hand. Tacking thread can be used since the stitches are temporary and will be removed after the seam is permanently stitched. A straight stitch is used for gathering by machine. The sewing machine should be set to the longest stitch, so the stitches are easy to gather and remove at the end.

1   Sew along the seam line of the section to be gathered, leaving a free length of thread at each end. Work another row of stitches ¼in (6mm) inside the seam allowance.

2   Pull a thread from each row at the same time to gather one half of the section. Insert a pin in the fabric and secure the threads by winding them in a figure of eight around it. Repeat for the other side to fit the required measurement.

3   Pin the gathered edge to the piece to be joined, matching notches, any seams and relevant markings. Adjust the gathers so that they are even between the pins. Remove the gathering stitches only after the seams have been permanently stitched.

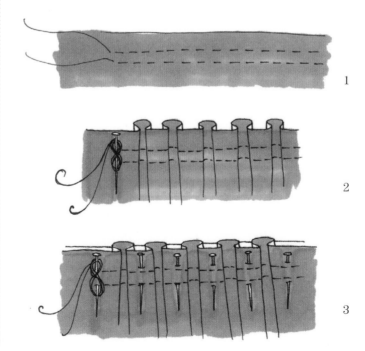

1

2

3

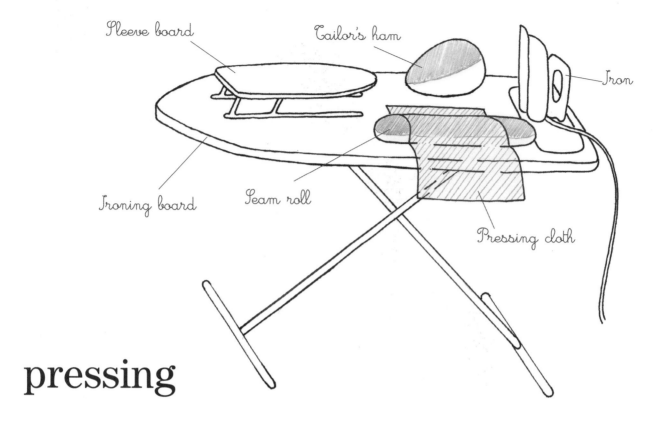

Sleeve board

Tailor's ham

Iron

Ironing board

Seam roll

Pressing cloth

pressing

Taking time to press the seams as you stitch them will help complete each stage of the project with ease as well as achieving a neat and professional finish.

Pressing equipment

Have all the equipment for pressing close by and set up ready to use. Press each seam and dart as you finish stitching.

Ironing board

Set up the ironing board at a height you are comfortable standing at.

Iron

The iron should have adjustable heat settings and a choice of steam or heat only. Use the point of the iron to open seams. Steam produces the right amount of moisture to set a collar or lapel and will make a crisp edge and flat seam. Use a dry cloth if applying the iron directly. If the iron is held away when steaming, a cloth is not required.

Pressing cloth

Press on the wrong side using a damp or dry cloth, if necessary, to protect the fabric from the heat of the iron and prevent shine. Muslin makes a good pressing cloth since it is see-through and can be used in a single layer or folded to adapt to the weight of the material you are pressing.

Sleeve board

A sleeve board is useful for pressing sleeve seams and other parts that will not fit on the ironing board.

Seam roll

This is a long, fabric-covered roll, which is used for pressing seams.

Tailor's ham

This is a shaped cushion that is firmly stuffed and ideal for pressing curved areas and darts.

To make a tailor's ham:

1 Cut an oval-shaped pattern from paper measuring around 12 x 9in (30 x 23cm). From the pattern cut two oval shapes in a firm calico cotton or wool.

2 With right sides together, stitch around the outside edge allowing a seam of ⅝in (1.5cm) and leaving an opening. Work a second line of stitching close to the first to reinforce the seam. Trim the seams and clip the curves.

3 Turn right sides out. Stuff very firmly with fine sawdust. Toy stuffing will not be firm enough. Pour the sawdust through a cone rolled from paper or thin card.

4 Turn in the raw edges and hand stitch the opening together with strong, doubled thread.

Key

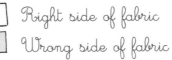

☐ Right side of fabric
▨ Wrong side of fabric

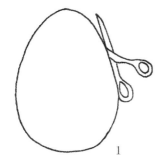

1

2

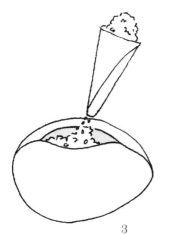

3

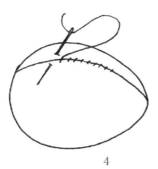

4

Pressing fabrics

Pressing is not the same as ironing. The iron is set down onto the fabric and then lifted, rather than pulled across the fabric. Set the iron to the right temperature for the fabric and test on a scrap first.

Cotton

A hot iron over a damp cloth will remove any creases.

Linen

Press with a hot iron on the wrong side of the fabric.

Silk

Press with a medium heat, using a dry cloth to avoid the seam line marking the right side of the fabric. Using a damp cloth may cause water marks.

Synthetics

Use a cool iron, avoiding going over the seams as this can mark the fabric. Do not dampen the material, but pass a steam iron over the fabric without touching it with the iron.

Wool

Use a warm iron and damp cloth. Leave on the board to dry naturally.

Velvet

Fabric with a pile should not be pressed directly. Press as little as possible and only on the back of the fabric, placing the pile side down on a needle board or onto the pile side of an oddment. Velvet can be steamed, taking care not to get it wet. Stand the iron upright and cover it with a damp cloth. Gently pass the velvet in front of the steam it produces to remove wrinkles.

decoration & finishing touches

A bound buttonhole, decorative edging or a little embroidery can enhance a piece of handmade clothing or an accessory. The extra detail and time spent will make your finished project truly special.

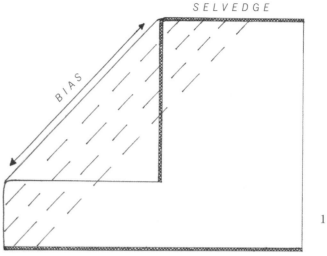

1

Bias binding

Bias binding provides a neat finish as well as strengthening and concealing raw edges. It is widely available to buy with ready-pressed edges, making it simple to apply. However, it is easy to make using your own choice of fabric.

1   Find the bias of the fabric by folding it diagonally at one end. Mark the fabric with diagonal lines, parallel to the bias fold. The lines should be the desired width of your binding with an extra ¼in (6mm) each side for the seams.

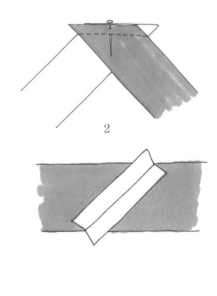

2

2   The short ends, which are cut on the grain, will be diagonal. With right sides together, pin and stitch the short ends together and press the seam open.

3   Fold both long edges in to the centre and press.

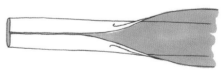

3

Binding outward corners

1 Open out one of the pressed edges of the binding
  and, with right side of binding to the wrong side
  of the garment, pin in place. Stitch along the seam to
  the corner, stopping at the seam line. Run the machine
  back and forth over a few stitches to reinforce the seam.

2 Fold the binding around the corner, aligning the fold
  with the edge just stitched. Pin and stitch the binding
  right along the adjoining edge of the corner. This will
  create a mitred edge on the right side of the binding.

3 Turn the binding to the right side of the garment,
  folding it at the corner so the mitre faces the opposite
  direction from the one on the inside. Pin over the seams
  and topstitch in place close to the edges, pivoting the
  needle at the corners.

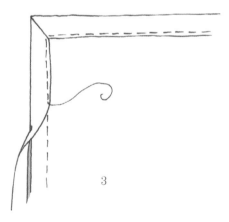

Buttonholes

Most of the projects in this book are fastened with buttons. The machine-worked buttonhole is a quick and easy method. The bound and hand-stitched buttonholes do take longer but will produce a beautiful finish to a garment.

Machine-worked buttonhole

Modern machines often have an automatic buttonhole attachment. However, a neat buttonhole can be produced using the zigzag stitch. This buttonhole is worked when the facings are already attached. Mark the position of the buttonholes. Take care to keep the lines straight and the stitches close together. At each end, the stitches should be wider than those down each side of the length. Cut the opening after stitching, using buttonhole scissors.

Machine-worked buttonhole

Hand-worked buttonhole

Mark the position of the buttonholes before you start. Make sure your stitches are even and close together.

1   Work a row of stitches by machine ⅛in (3mm) on each side and across both ends of the buttonhole marking. Carefully cut the length of the buttonhole with sharp scissors.

2   With the right side of the work facing, stitch around the edges by inserting the needle through the cut line and out just beyond the line of stitching. Keep the thread under the point of the needle and draw the needle up to tighten the thread, forming a little knot at the cut edge. Keep the stitches evenly spaced and equal in length.

3   Fan the stitches around the end towards the opening of the garment and work a straight bar of stitches at the other end to prevent the buttonhole from splitting.

Hand-worked buttonhole

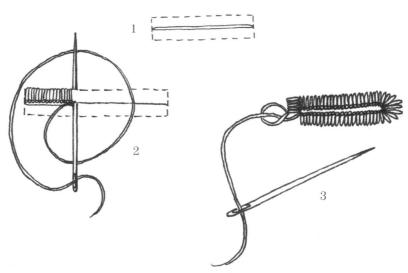

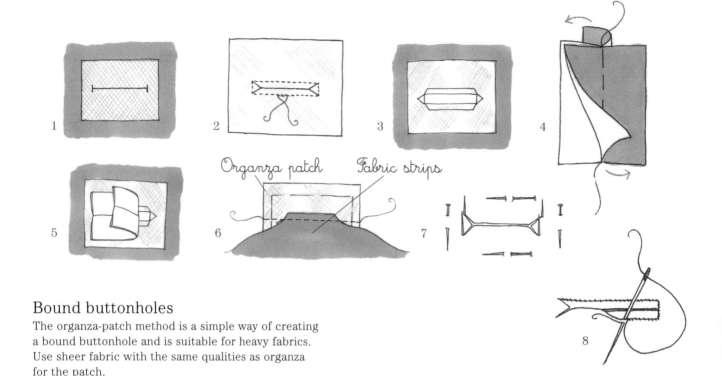

Organza patch   Fabric strips

Bound buttonholes

The organza-patch method is a simple way of creating
a bound buttonhole and is suitable for heavy fabrics.
Use sheer fabric with the same qualities as organza
for the patch.

1   Transfer the buttonhole markings
    from the pattern to the front
    (right front for girls and left front
    for boys) using a tailor's chalk
    pencil. Cut a small patch of iron-on
    interfacing around 1in (2.5cm)
    larger than the buttonhole. Apply
    it to the wrong side of the fabric
    where each buttonhole will be
    positioned, to reinforce the area.

2   Cut the patch of fabric 2in
    (5cm) longer and wider than the
    buttonhole. Pin in place on the
    right side of the garment, centred
    over the buttonhole marking. Work
    a line of short stitches, ¼in (6mm)
    from each side of the marking
    and across the ends, starting and
    finishing in the middle of one long
    edge and pivoting the needle at the
    corners. Carefully cut the opening
    through all thicknesses to within
    ¼in (6mm) of the ends, taking care
    not to go through the stitches.
    Snip the fabric diagonally into the
    corners of the stitching.

3   Turn the patch to the wrong side
    and press flat so seam allowances
    lay away from the opening, creating
    a window.

4   To make the lips of the buttonhole,
    cut two strips of the main fabric
    1½in (4cm) longer and wider
    than the buttonhole. With right
    sides together, tack the two strips
    together along the centre. Press
    the seam open.

5   On the wrong side, position the
    strip evenly so the seam runs
    across the middle of the opening
    and pin in place close to each end.

6   Stitch the strips to the long seam
    allowances along the previous line
    of stitches, extending the stitching
    across both ends of the organza and
    strips to secure. Stitch the strips
    to the short edges in the same way.
    Finish sewing the garment before
    continuing.

Facing

7   Pin the facing or lining in place
    around the bound buttonhole. Push
    a pin through each corner from the
    right side to mark the size of the
    buttonhole. Cut a slit in the facing
    or lining to correspond with the
    oblong shape on the right side of
    the buttonhole, snipping diagonally
    into the corners.

8   Turn under the raw edges of the
    facing and hem in place. Remove
    the tacking stitches and press well.

Buttons

Many buttons have a shank, a raised part underneath it, allowing room for thickness of the fabric around the buttonhole. Buttons without a shank need to be attached in such a way as to form a shank with the thread, so that they are easy to fasten and sit neatly on the fabric. Use thread coated with beeswax *(see page 141)* to sew the buttons to the garment.

1   Mark the position of the button on the fabric. For horizontal buttonholes, the position of the shank should be near the end closest to the opening. For vertical buttonholes, the shank should be central.

2   Secure the thread to the fabric. Place a matchstick or hairgrip over the button and work over it when sewing the button. When the button feels secure, remove the matchstick.

3   Pull the needle through so that the thread lies between the button and the fabric. Slide the button to the top of the stitches and wind the thread around the stitches under the button to form a shank. Work some stitches through the shank and fasten off securely on the wrong side of the fabric.

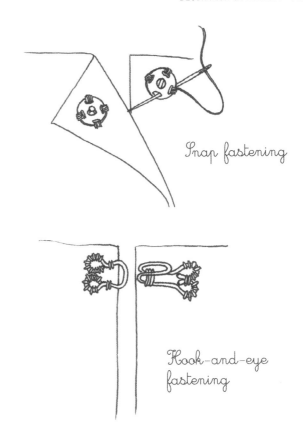

Snap fastening

Hook-and-eye fastening

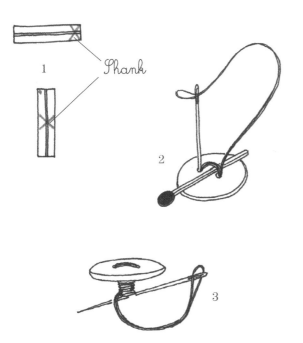

Snap fastening

Stitch the ball half of the snap fastening to the underside of the overlap, working several small stitches over each other through each hole. Carry the thread from one hole to the next, under the snap. To mark the position of the socket half, rub tailor's chalk onto the ball of the snap and place against the fabric where it will be fastened. Stitch the socket half of the snap in position.

Hook-and-eye fastening

For a closure that meets, as on the party dress on page 88, the hook and eye should be stitched to the inside of the garment. Sew the hook to the right-hand side of the opening, working several small stitches over each other through each hole. Sew the end of the hook to the garment to hold it flat. Stitch the rounded eye to the left-hand side so it extends slightly beyond the edge of the garment, sewing a few stitches to each side of the eye to hold it down.

Appliqué

Appliqué is featured on the boy's pants on page 78, bib on page 130 and pirate hat on page 104. Fusible web interfacing (see page 145) is used to bond the fabrics. A paper backing covers one of the fusible sides.

1   Trace the design onto the paper side of the interfacing. (Remember to reverse the image if using your own design). Place the shiny side down onto the wrong side of the fabric and iron for a few seconds to bond.

2   Cut the design out, following the lines drawn on the paper, and then remove the backing paper.

3   Position the fusible side down on the right side of the garment and press under a damp cloth, as with iron-on interfacing. Leave to cool before stitching.

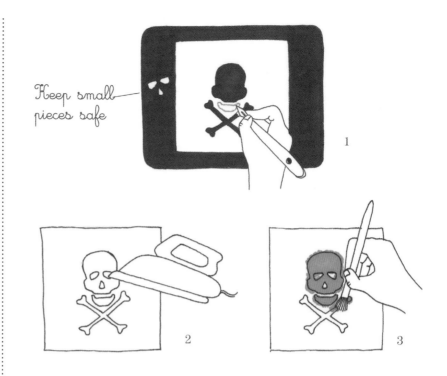

Keep small pieces safe

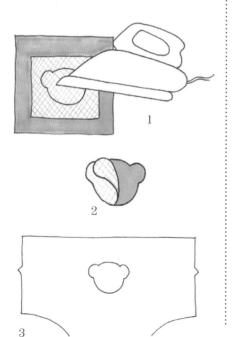

Freezer-paper stencils

Stencils decorate the crown and tabard on pages 102 and 109. Freezer paper is used to preserve food, but is ideal for sewing projects as well.

1   Trace the design onto the paper side of the freezer paper. Using a sharp craft knife on a cutting mat, carefully cut out the design from the freezer paper. Any small details, such as the eyes and nose of the skull, should be kept in a safe place until you are ready to use them.

2   With the shiny side down, fuse the freezer-paper stencil in place on the fabric with a hot iron, including any small pieces. Concentrate particularly around the edges of the design, using the tip of the iron, to ensure the stencil has adhered to the fabric.

3   Place newspaper underneath the fabric so the paint doesn't stain the work surface. Using a paintbrush, dab the colour through the cut-away areas onto the fabric. Use a very small amount of fabric paint at a time to build up the colour, taking care not to push the paint under the edges of the stencil. Leave the freezer paper in place until the fabric paint is dry. Fix the design by placing a dry cloth over the top and ironing well for a few minutes on both sides at the highest heat suitable for the fabric.

Buttonhole stitch

Chain stitch

Straight stitch

Embroidery stitches

The following embroidery stitches are used to decorate the animal masks, toys and appliquéd pants on pages 114, 122 and 78, giving them a personal finishing touch.

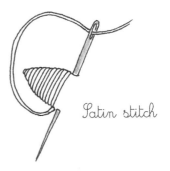

Satin stitch

Buttonhole stitch

On the right side of the work, insert the needle above the line of the design and bring it out on the line itself. Pass the thread under the point of the needle. Draw the needle through the loop, making the stitch tight but taking care not to pucker the fabric. Continue in this way, keeping the stitches the same length and evenly spaced.

Chain stitch

Bring the thread through to the right side of the work at the position where the stitch is to be made and hold it down with your left thumb. Insert the needle where it first came out and bring it back through a little way from the last point, according to the length of the stitch you wish to make. Pull through, keeping the thread under the needle. Repeat to continue the chain.

Satin stitch

Work straight stitches side by side and close together across a shape. Take care to keep the stitches even and the edge neat. The finished result will look like satin.

Straight stitch

This is a single stitch that can be worked in varying lengths. It is useful for embroidering short lines.

Cross stitch

1   Bring the needle through to the front of the work, then take the first stitch diagonally from right to left, bringing the needle back through in line with the point where the first stitch emerged.

2   Complete the cross stitch by inserting the needle back through the work in line with the top of the previous stitch, from left to right.

Cross stitch

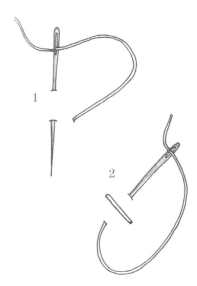

templates

Trace the chosen template onto tracing paper.
Slip dressmaker's carbon paper, carbon side down,
between the template and the right side of the fabric
and trace over with a pencil to transfer the design.

Pants appliqué template

Bib templates

Tabard and pirate
hat templates

garment sizes

Children vary in size, so it is very important to take their measurements before starting a project in order to get a better fit.

To help choose the correct size, please refer to the chart below.

AGE	6 MONTHS	1 YEAR	2 YEARS	3 YEARS
Height	26½in (68cm)	34in (86cm)	38½in (98cm)	41in (104cm)
Back to waist	7½in (19cm)	8in (20.5cm)	8½in (21.5cm)	9in (23cm)
Chest	19in (48.5cm)	20in (51cm)	21in (53.5cm)	22in (55.5cm)
Waist	19in (48.5cm)	19½in (49.5cm)	20in (51cm)	20½in (52cm)
Hip	20in (51cm)	21in (53.5cm)	22in (55.5cm)	23in (58cm)
Outside leg	13½in (34.5cm)	18in (45.75cm)	22½in (57cm)	25in (64cm)

How to read the 'Fabric Required' charts

Follow the cutting layouts provided at the beginning of the larger projects. This will ensure the most efficient use of the fabric you have chosen. The length of fabric required can be found on the chart accompanying each project, where applicable. As fabric comes in various widths, the amount needed is given for three different fabric widths. Select the measurement appropriate to the child's size and the width of fabric that you have chosen.

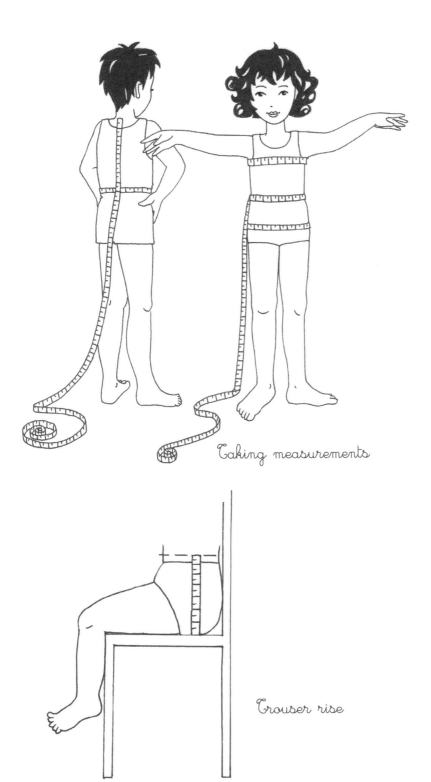

Taking measurements

Trouser rise

Taking measurements

When taking width measurements, make sure that the tape is parallel to the floor and held taut, but not tight, against the body.

Chest: Measure under the arms, over the fullest part of the chest and straight across the back.

Waist: Tie a length of string or ribbon around the child's waist to find their natural waistline and measure over the string.

Hip: Measure around the fullest part of the hip, below the waistline.

Back waist length: Measure from the nape, the prominent bone at the back of the neck, down to the waist.

Outside leg: Take this measurement at the side, from the waistline to the floor or down to the desired skirt or trouser length.

The following measurements are useful when making trousers:

Trouser rise: This is the length of the crotch. With the child sitting on a chair, take a measurement from the side of the waist to the seat of the chair. The inside-leg measurement will be the difference between the crotch length and the outside-leg measurement. To check the trouser-rise measurement against that of the pattern, measure near the side seam from the widest part of the crotch to the waist. The measurements should match with ½–1in (1.25–2.5cm) extra allowed for sitting ease.

resources

Fabric

Australia

The Fabric Store
21 Cooper Street
Surry Hills
New South Wales 2010
Tel: +61 (0) 292 112217
Email: sydney@thefabricstore.com.au
www.thefabricstore.com.au

France

Tissus Reine
3–5 Place St Pierre
75018 Paris
www.tissus-reine.com

Japan

Habu Textiles Kyoto
36 Nishi-machi
Honen-in
Shishigatani
Sakyo-ku
Kyoto 606-8427
Tel: +81 (0) 75 762 2251
Email: habutextileskyoto@gmail.com
www.habutextiles.com

UK

Ditto Fabrics
21 Kensington Gardens
Brighton
East Sussex
BN1 4AL
Tel: +44 (0) 1273 958959
Email: sales@dittofabrics.co.uk
www.dittofabrics.co.uk

Eclectic Maker
13 Station Parade
Tarring Road
Worthing
BN11 4SS
Tel: +44 (0) 845 862 5552
Email: customer.service@
eclecticmaker.co.uk
www.eclecticmaker.co.uk

MacCulloch & Wallis
25–26 Dering Street
London
W1S 1AT
Tel: +44 (0) 20 7629 0311
Email: samples@macculloch.com
www.macculloch-wallis.co.uk

Merchant & Mills Limited
14A Tower Street
Rye
East Sussex
TN31 7AT
Tel: +44 (0) 1797 227789
www.merchantandmills.com

Ray Stitch
99 Essex Road
London
N1 2SJ
Tel: +44 (0) 20 7704 1060
Email: info@raystitch.co.uk
www.raystitch.co.uk

The Stitchery
12–16 Riverside
Cliffe Bridge
High Street
Lewes
East Sussex
BN7 2RE
Tel: +44 (0) 1273 473577
Email: info@the-stitchery.co.uk
www.the-stitchery.co.uk

USA

Brooklyn General Store
128 Union Street
Brooklyn
New York 11231
Tel: +1 718 237 7753
www.brooklyngeneral.com

Habu Textiles
135 West 29th Street
Suite 804
New York 10001
Tel: +1 212 239 3546
Email: habu@habutextiles.com
www.habutextiles.com

Purl Soho
459 Broome Street
New York, 10013
Tel: +1 212 420 8796
www.purlsoho.com

Sewing Tools
and Haberdashery

Australia

Lincraft
41–59 O'Riordan Street
Alexandria
New South Wales 2015
Tel: +61 (0) 296 691168
www.lincraft.com.au

Japan

Habu Textiles Kyoto
(see opposite)

UK

Ernest Wright and Son Limited
Endeavour Works
58 Broad Lane
Sheffield
S1 4BT
Tel: +44 (0) 1142 754812
Email: enquiries@ernestwright.co.uk
www.ernestwright.co.uk

MacCulloch & Wallis
(see opposite)

Merchant & Mills Limited
(see opposite)

Ray Stitch
(see opposite)

Tailor Mouse Limited
Claro Court Business Park
Claro Road
Harrogate
North Yorkshire
HG1 4BA
Tel: +44 (0) 1423 819425
www.tailormouse.co.uk

The Stitchery
(see opposite)

Wayward
68 Norman Road
St Leonards-on-sea
East Sussex
TN38 OEJ
Tel: +44 (0) 78 1501 3337
Email: info@wayward.co
www.wayward.co

USA

Brooklyn General Store
(see opposite)

Habu Textiles
(see opposite)

Purl Soho
(see opposite)

Embroidery threads

France

Renaissance Dyeing
Andie Luijk
place Théophile Delcasse
09600, Montbel d'en Bas
Ariège
Tel: +33 (0) 4 6831 5323
www.renaissancedyeing.com

UK

Appleton Brothers Ltd
Thames Works
Church Street
Chiswick
W4 2PE
Tel: +44 (0) 20 8994 0711
www.embroiderywool.co.uk

Hobbycraft
Customer Services
Hobbycraft DC
E-Commerce Door A
Parkway
Centrum 100 Business Park, Unit 1
Burton Upon Trent
DE14 2WA
Tel: +44 (0) 330 026 1400
www.hobbycraft.co.uk

The Stitchery
(see opposite)

USA

Purl Soho
(see opposite)

acknowledgements

Author's acknowledgements
I would like to thank Jonathan Bailey for giving me the opportunity to write *Sew Adorable*. Thank you to Virginia Brehaut, Rebecca Mothersole and all at GMC, and a special thank you to Sara Harper and Cath Senker for all of your support and patience. For their endless encouragement, I wish to thank my husband Damian and my children Miriam, Dilys, Flynn and Honey.

I would like to dedicate this book to my granddaughter, Dolly, for being my mannequin, patiently letting me adjust the patterns while she modelled them, when all she really wanted to do was run off into her own creative and magical world of adventure.

Publisher's acknowledgements
GMC Publications would like to thank Hope Knight at the Tin Tabernacle, Barcombe; Amelia Holmwood and Vanessa Mooncie for their help at the photo shoot and Laura Holmwood for the loan of props.

Thanks also to the following toddlers and to their mummies and daddies for allowing us to photograph them for this book: Cressida, Dolly, Evje, Florence, Jack, Lulin, Rocky and Tai.

index

To place an order, or to request a catalogue, contact:
GMC Publications Ltd
Castle Place, 166 High Street, Lewes, East Sussex, BN7 1XU
United Kingdom
Tel: +44 (0)1273 488005
www.gmcbooks.com